Cultivating a Learner-Centered Classroom

Cultivating
the Learner-Centered
Classroom
From Theory to Practice

Kaia Tollefson • Monica K. Osborn

CORWIN PRESS
A SAGE Company
Thousand Oaks, CA 91320

For information:

Corwin Press
A SAGE Company
2455 Teller Road
Thousand Oaks, California 91320
www.corwinpress.com

SAGE Ltd.
1 Oliver's Yard
55 City Road
London EC1Y 1SP
United Kingdom

SAGE India Pvt. Ltd.
B 1/I 1 Mohan Cooperative
   Industrial Area
Mathura Road, New Delhi 110 044
India

SAGE Asia-Pacific Pte. Ltd.
33 Pekin Street #02-01
Far East Square
Singapore 048763

Printed in the United States of America.

Library of Congress Cataloging-in-Publication Data

Tollefson, Kaia.
Cultivating the learner-centered classroom: from theory to practice/Kaia Tollefson, Monica K. Osborn.
      p. cm.
Includes bibliographical references and index.
ISBN 978-1-4129-4996-5 (cloth)
ISBN 978-1-4129-4997-2 (pbk.)
    1. Active learning. 2. Individualized instruction. 3. Constructivism (Education)
4. Classroom environment—United States. I. Osborn, Monica K. II. Title.

LB1027.23.T65 2008
371.39—dc22   2007024751

This book is printed on acid-free paper.

07   08   09   10   11   10 9 8 7 6 5 4 3 2 1

Acquisitions Editor:	Cathy Hernandez
Editorial Assistants:	Megan Bedell, Cathleen Mortensen
Production Editor:	Eric Garner
Copy Editor:	Paula L. Fleming
Typesetter:	C&M Digitals (P) Ltd.
Proofreader:	Kevin Gleason
Indexer:	Sheila Bodell
Cover Designer:	Lisa Miller

Contents

Preface

"Veronica gets it!" Allison said about one of the first-year teachers who had been hired to teach first grade at her school. She continued, sharing a perfectly simple story to illustrate the complexity of what "getting it" means to her.

"When I walked into Veronica's classroom on the first day of school, I saw that she had already posted 40 or 50 words on the word wall. Her room looked so great, and I didn't have the heart to point out that small problem—that since the need for those spelling words hadn't come from her kids, they probably wouldn't ever know what the word wall was about or how they could use it to help with their writing. But then last week I went in, and she had taken all of her words down. I asked her about it, and she said she'd noticed that her kids weren't ever using the word wall. She'd decided that for it to be useful for her students, the words had to be ones that they were actually using in their writing but didn't know how to spell yet. She'd decided that they had to build their word wall together.

"I was so impressed with that! As a first-year teacher, she was paying enough attention to what her students were showing her that she could say, 'I noticed they weren't using it.' And she could take this idea that she'd learned about in college and make it real by watching what her kids did with it. She gets it!"

Veronica is a promising new teacher. She understands what the phrase "student-centered" means in the real life of her classroom. Unfortunately, real life for Veronica also means that she is working 10- to 12-hour days and never feeling finished. Her classroom is artfully organized and is wonderfully warm, inviting, and kid-friendly—but she is tired and stressed and often seems to be running on willpower alone. One of Veronica's best friends has already quit his first teaching job, joining the ranks of the nearly 50% of new teachers who leave the profession within the first five years of their careers (National Education Association, 2006). Veronica "gets it," but the hard fact is that there's little better than a 50–50 chance that she'll still be teaching in ten years. She gets it, which means that while she understands why student-centered theories shape her ideas about what it means to be a teacher, she knows, now, that making this approach work is one of the most difficult challenges she will ever face. We hope this book will be of use for helping teachers like Veronica to put those theories to work in the classroom.

If you know what it feels like to struggle for balance between what you believe and what you can accomplish in the classroom, or if you've had the dismal experience of watching your ideals diminish into the distance as you fight to keep from drowning in the realities of day-to-day life at school, you're not alone. Virtually every teacher we know believes in a number of student-centered ideas about what it means to teach and to learn; yet in our experience, many tend to be more learner-centered philosophically than in practice. For some, this may be because they are not yet as confident as they want to be about how to do things like individualize instruction, engage different intelligences and learning styles, or facilitate the development of a strong and supportive community for learning. For others—and for new teachers in particular, many of whom may be working in "failing" schools in some of the most challenging conditions imaginable—the unambiguous message often heard is that the reality of test scores will trump student-centered ideals every time and that instructional efforts need to be more precisely focused on standards than on students. In such a climate, growing into one's potential as an effective, learner-centered educator can be more difficult than ever, since time—every teacher's most precious resource—is often increasingly controlled by those who are not actually responsible for doing the work of teaching and learning at the level of real life in the classroom. Whatever the reason, one thing is clear: learning how to connect genuinely with kids and to teach them well takes time.

TIME TO LEARN

With coaching from experienced others, we learn to swim by swimming and to read by reading. It follows that we learn to teach by teaching. Unfortunately, guided opportunities to learn by teaching tend to be woefully insufficient for new and experienced educators alike. The student teaching experience, while essential, cannot provide in a few semesters what will take years to learn; yet once licensed and hired, teachers are typically, illogically left mostly alone to become the deeply reflective, challenging, confident, and child-centered practitioners that they were probably encouraged to be in their credentialing programs. While the theoretical preparation for the classroom that many teacher education programs provide is essential for helping students of education to understand *why* learner-centered theories are important, the *how* of this approach to teaching cannot be fully learned in a university environment, nor in a 16- or 32-week internship. Undergraduate and graduate students in education can learn about the theories of constructivism, multiple intelligences, learning styles, developmentally appropriate practice, and motivation, for example; but such theories hold real meaning only for teachers who have first implemented various strategies that embody these ideas, then tested those strategies by trial and error, day after day and year after year.

Figuring out how to translate learner-centered theories of education into everyday classroom practice can be a discouraging process, even in schools where external pressures to standardize teaching and learning are minimized and in which strong mentoring programs and genuine collegial opportunities for all teachers exist. Without consistent mentoring and other supports, though, the struggle to hold onto student-centered ideals—the ones that made such obvious sense in a college classroom—can be overwhelming for both new and experienced educators. For these teachers, the serious challenge of every day can become that of simply surviving it. Alana, a strong and highly capable young woman who recently completed her first year in the classroom, describes what she survived. "I worked 12-hour days all year, including at least one day on the weekend," she said, "and I cried my way home, every night." When asked what she wishes for now that her first year is behind her, she says simply, "I just wish I had more time with my kids." From listening to Alana talk about her goals as a new teacher, it is clear that she made it to the end of the year with her ideals intact. It is equally clear that the emotional toll along the way was high.

FIGHTING FOR HOPE

The sense of disconnection between educational theory and real life in the schools can be professionally and personally debilitating. Untold numbers of the nation's 3 million teachers work fiercely every day to cultivate a child-centered, constructivist pedagogy, often in the face of great financial, social, political, and institutional barriers. Others learn to cope by abandoning the progressive philosophy of education they had once embraced in favor of the teacher-centered strategies of behaviorism (i.e., the prediction and control of students' observable behaviors), which tend to be simpler and easier to implement than the student-centered strategies of constructivism. It seems probable that at least some of the 1,000 teachers who leave the profession every school day in the United States (Alliance for Excellent Education, 2005) do so because they lack support in learning how to put deeply held beliefs about what it should mean to teach and to learn into practice. Hope is at stake. It is our newest colleagues and our most fragile student populations who are living on the front lines of a devastating teacher attrition rate that reveals two clear trends: attrition is "roughly 50 percent higher in poor schools than in wealthier ones," and "teachers new to the profession are far more likely to leave than are their more experienced counterparts" (Alliance for Excellent Education, 2005, p. 2).

It is clear from where we sit that years of school reform and accountability efforts have not inspired hope. They have not made classrooms more enticing places for teachers or students to want to be. Instead, they have contributed to a profound disconnect between child-centered pedagogy and real life in many schools. This book is intended for teachers who have felt the uncomfortable, even painful divide between their philosophical beliefs and the realities of day-to-day life in the schools. It is also intended for administrators and classroom mentors who are devoted to supporting others' growth, as well as their own, toward the goal of integrating learner-centered theory and practice—despite the many real and varied pressures they are under to abandon a constructivist ideology.

It is important to acknowledge what we see as an unfortunate reality for those who value learner-centered schools and classrooms (which we define as genuine learning communities in which all students, parents, and educators feel safe, valuable, and capable enough to risk engaging their real selves in their experiences at school): we are working against the dominant paradigm of behaviorism—that is, of predicting and controlling others' behaviors—when it comes to defining what it means to teach and to learn. Going against the norm is always hard, but it can seem next to impossible alone. It's *hard* to resist falling back on deeply engrained habits and strategies (or on the worksheet packets helpfully offered by the well-intended teacher next door) when we are not immediately successful in helping our students to be the respectful, inquisitive, courageous, and capable learners we want them to be. This is particularly true when our students are old enough to know very well how school is *supposed* to work, with minimal investment of effort and courage on their part and with responsibility for control being solely the teacher's concern.

This book, then, is written for teachers who want to be more genuinely student-centered in their classrooms, who have discovered important questions about their practice and who look forward to finding more, and who are willing to make mistakes and try new things every day to figure out how to engage students' real selves in their learning. It is intended to help both new and experienced teachers with these goals by offering concrete strategies for making a fundamental shift in educational thought and practice: from behaviorism to constructivism; from control to cooperation; from achieving standardized, age-based expectations for students' development to using standards for individualizing expectations and instruction; and from coercing students' obedience to facilitating their authority and autonomy. In short, the book provides educators with ideas for ensuring that the processes of education are done *by* the students in our care rather than *to* them.

In the upcoming chapters, we offer our best "how-to" thinking about teaching, and we do our best to show how the strategies described are aligned with learner-centered ideas about education. We do so, knowing from experience that it is possible to maintain the sturdy sense of authority that students need their teachers to have while sharing power with them, purposefully helping them to develop the sense of agency and authority that every engaged citizen requires. We want to be clear, though, that while our own teaching experiences in New Mexico and Alaska have been in settings characterized by great cultural and socioeconomic diversity, largely in Title I schools serving poor families and neighborhoods, we recognize the distinction between teaching children who are poor and teaching those who live in chronic, generational poverty. We do not speak from experience in working with large numbers of children and parents who are living in deeply impoverished circumstances. While we believe the student-centered theories and practical strategies we describe are effective and beneficial for all learners, we do not presume to know, in fact, what our teaching colleagues in America's most impoverished schools and neighborhoods know better. Further, we appreciate the cultural chasms that significantly define the educational landscape when teaching "other people's children" (Delpit, 2006), and as white women who are economically privileged, by world standards, we recognize the limits of our perspectives and understandings. We simply offer these approaches for critique, hoping they'll be of use for teachers who are also interested in finding ways to put students at the center of our conversations, our practices, and our profession.

The melding of theory and practice is our goal in describing the following aspects of teaching: (Chapter 1) facilitating community development in the classroom; (Chapter 2) classroom organization; (Chapter 3) observing and assessing what students know and can do; (Chapter 4) planning instruction; (Chapter 5) evaluating and reporting student growth; (Chapter 6) facilitating community development with parents; and (Chapter 7) leading with heart.

These topics are relevant for teachers at every grade level and are described in general rather than age-specific terms. We trust readers to modify and apply these ideas as needed in a variety of settings. We hope that this text (and the conversations it can provoke with colleagues, parents, and students) will help to strengthen your own learning community and to provoke ongoing and justifiable optimism as you continue the challenge of putting learner-centered theories to work in your classroom. You will be doing such important work with the hundreds of children who will be in your care over the course of your career. May you inspire each one.

Acknowledgments

So many people have shaped our ideas about what it means to be learner centered, most significantly the educators and authors whose work we've cited and our students from the Rio Rancho Public School District, California State University Channel Islands, the University of New Mexico, and the Kodiak Island Borough School District. Our sincere thanks go to them, as well as to Merilyn Buchanan, Keli Carlin, Jessica Chavez, Christina Chavez-Apodaca, Rose Ebaugh, Jane Erlandson, Jeanne Grier, Maria Hines, Margaret Kavanaugh, Liz Keefe, Mary Linscheid, Gilberto Lobo-Martinez, Lisa Moore, Kelley Peters, Judy Reagan, Kristi Sackett, Charlotte Stocek, and Kamara Yri—our friends, colleagues, and family members who shared their ideas, critiqued portions of this text as they were being drafted, and pushed our thinking about what it means to be learner centered. Finally, we thank Cathy Hernandez, our editor at Corwin Press, who guided us so gracefully through this project.

Corwin Press gratefully acknowledges the contributions of the following reviewers:

Christene Alfonsi, Tenth Grade English Teacher
Fairfield Senior High School, Oxford, OH

Gwen Childs, First Grade Teacher
Vestavia Hills Elementary School-East, Vestavia Hills, AL

Elizabeth F. Day, Sixth GradeTeacher
Mechanicville Middle School, Mechanicville, NY

Kathleen Kesson, Professor of Urban Childhood Education
Long Island University, Brooklyn, NY

Amanda Linn, Art Teacher
Parkview Arts and Science Magnet High School, Little Rock, AR

Deborah Meier, Adjunct Professor of Teaching and Learning
New York University, New York, NY

E. Wayne Ross, Professor of Curriculum Studies
University of British Columbia, Vancouver, BC

Joe Underwood, Entertainment Arts Teacher
Miami High School, Miami, FL

Jennifer Wong, Third Grade Teacher
Edward Gideon School, Philadelphia, PA

About the Authors

The authors have over three decades of combined experience in education, experience that between the two includes twenty-three years of classroom teaching, six years in administration, and eight years in higher education. Additionally, they have worked as educational consultants at local, state, and national levels and together share sixteen years of experience in mentoring and supervising student teachers. Their collaboration began in 1998, when they shared responsibility for the same students: Monica mentored student teachers in her multiage classroom whom Kaia served as a supervisor and methods instructor.

 **Kaia Tollefson**'s career in education began in Kodiak, Alaska, in 1983. She was a middle school teacher there for nine years and worked in administration for the next five—first as a curriculum and staff development coordinator and then as an elementary school principal. She discovered a passion for teacher education while pursuing her doctoral degree in language, literacy, and sociocultural studies, awarded by the University of New Mexico in 2004. Her most recent experience in teaching children was in 2002, when she returned to the classroom to teach fifth grade. One of her professional goals is to find ways to refresh and reground her roots in the public schools, never getting too far away from knowing what it means to be a classroom teacher. She is currently an assistant professor of education at California State University Channel Islands, working in teacher education, coaching a Critical Friends Group, and exploring the relationship between the concept of voice and the processes of teaching and learning.

 **Monica K. Osborn** has been teaching at Puesta del Sol Elementary School in Rio Rancho, New Mexico, since 1994. She earned her bachelor's and master's degrees in education from the University of New Mexico in 1994 and 1995, respectively, and an education specialist degree in educational leadership in 2007. She is a certified Reading Recovery teacher, currently teaching grades K–2 in a multiage inclusion classroom. She is also certified through the National Board for Professional Teaching Standards and is recognized as a Level III teacher-leader in the state of New Mexico. In addition to her work as a classroom teacher, Monica serves as an educational consultant with the New Mexico Education Network Center and with the National School Reform Faculty, specializing in facilitating the implementation of Critical Friends Groups (CFGs), professional learning communities for educators. She is a CFG coach at her school and has been teaching the process to teachers and administrators in several regions of the United States for the past eight years.

Introduction

Progressivism and Traditionalism: A Continuum of Educational Thought

A number of how-to books on teaching are written in terms that reflect a kinship with behaviorism and an educational philosophy in which the value of uniformity is emphasized (i.e., the standardization of instructional and evaluation practices as well as the standardization of expectations for students' cognitive and social development by any given age). Many of these more traditional texts do promote a number of progressive, child-centered strategies for teaching and learning, but they often attempt to fit those approaches into an ideological framework that presents the current trend toward standardization and the value of educational uniformity as inevitable and indisputable. Many urge teachers to adopt a positive attitude toward the "ideal" of mandated uniformity at the same time that they encourage the implementation of some progressive strategies in their teaching.

We do not believe that it is helpful to try to reconcile these fundamentally differing ideologies in this way. Traditional and progressive approaches to teaching are informed by vastly different beliefs and values about the purposes of schools and about how students learn, and that's a good thing. It should be acceptable for teachers—even those working next door to one another within the same school—to have differing ideas about education.

We recognize at the outset that phrases like *student-centered* and *progressive education* are used disparagingly by a number of prominent public school critics. We view such criticism as helpful and necessary—not only for ensuring that progressively oriented educators can clearly articulate why they embrace learner-centered theories and practices in

1

their classrooms but also to highlight what is at stake when intolerance for others' perspectives and methods is normed. Our belief is that in a genuinely democratic society, the creative tension between opposing ideas about such a crucial topic as the education of its children must be consciously welcomed and officially valued; for freedom to exist, there must be room for competing beliefs. The extent to which vigorous, respectful public debate is enjoyed is actually a telltale measure of social freedom and democratic integrity. This idea, we must remind ourselves, is equally relevant for those of us who are frustrated by "traditional" views about the appropriate ends and means of education.

From one perspective, then, education is seen primarily as the process of ensuring that all students are "on grade level" in terms of their ability to master a prescribed body of knowledge and skills by a certain age. The essential purpose of education in this traditional view is for all students to achieve established learning goals that are standardized by content area and by their age or grade level. Progressive educators, on the other hand, are more concerned with where students are in their development as readers, writers, mathematicians, and so on rather than with where they are supposed to be by a certain age. They are focused on identifying and building on students' strengths, keeping a constant eye on what is next for them to learn—which can be helpfully informed by established standards and benchmarks that define typical developmental progression, not age-based mandates, in the content areas.

In contrast to a school of thought that presents the need for standardization more visibly than the needs and progress of individual students, a progressive educator would argue that (1) students' needs must come before all others, existing as the central focus for every educational decision—whether those decisions are made at the corporate, federal, state, district, school, or classroom level (this hierarchical ordering reflects what we see as an egregious reality, that the farther an educational decision maker is from children, the more authority and power he has to define the ends and means of education); (2) strong language and math skills are the essential means for education rather than its end goal; and (3) the purpose of education, or the end goal, is to help students to discover and develop their talents to the fullest. This last idea is in keeping with a definition of education that comes from the Latin word *educere*, which means to bring out and to draw forth. From this perspective, education is for helping children to find their place in the world, to discover what their unique contributions to society might be. This is why motivation matters so much to learner-centered teachers: they believe that for students to want to learn and to do their best, they need to have a measure of control over their environments and activities (Deci & Koestner, 1999; Deci & Ryan, n.d., 1996, 2000; Kohn, 1993; Ryan & Deci, 2000; Sheldon & Biddle, 1998). The desire to achieve must come from within, but student-centered teachers understand that one of their most fundamental responsibilities—if not *the* most fundamental responsibility—is to cultivate and to nurture that desire.

From a student-centered point of view, a genuine desire to learn and to develop one's talents to the fullest is particularly important in the context of democracy. Educators at the John Dewey Project on Progressive Education (2002) at the University of Vermont explained:

> Although there are numerous differences of style and emphasis among progressive educators, they share the conviction that democracy means active participation by all citizens in social, political and economic decisions that will affect their lives. The education of engaged citizens, according to this perspective, involves two essential elements: (1) *Respect for diversity,* meaning that each individual should be recognized for his or her own abilities, interests, ideas, needs, and cultural identity, and (2) the development of *critical, socially engaged intelligence,* which enables individuals to understand and participate effectively in the affairs of their community in a collaborative effort to achieve a common good. (¶1)

While these ideas are presented to differentiate between traditional and progressive education, it is useful to note that these two words represent a continuum rather than a dichotomy in educational thought. A philosophical continuum (illustrated in Figures 0.1–0.5) can be defined in terms that represent distinctly different kinds of educational thought, from radical progressivism on the far left to radical traditionalism on the far right. We offer definitions for radical progressivism, moderate progressivism, moderate traditionalism, and radical traditionalism in five different areas in education: curriculum (Figure 0.1), accountability (Figure 0.2), standardization (Figure 0.3), motivation (Figure 0.4), and classroom/school environment (Figure 0.5). We do so believing it is possible for a person to occupy various positions on this continuum of educational thought, depending upon which aspect of education is under consideration. We, for example, are more moderate in the areas of curriculum and accountability than we are on the topics of standardization, motivation, and classroom/school environment. This book, then, is ideologically positioned between moderate and radical progressivism as we have defined those terms in Figures 0.1–0.5.

(text continues on page 8)

A CONTINUUM OF EDUCATIONAL THOUGHT

Figure 0.1   Curriculum

Radical Progressivism	Moderate Progressivism	Moderate Traditionalism	Radical Traditionalism
The curriculum must be developed at the classroom level, following the interests of the learners themselves. Any imposition of curriculum or standards from outside of the classroom is seen as an objectification of learners and teachers. Curriculum derives entirely from the idea that education is appropriately defined through the Latin term, educere (to bring forth, to draw out).	The curriculum can be created at the classroom, district, and state level. District- and state-level standards and benchmarks provide a suggested (not required) organizational framework for educators, particularly helpful for (1) beginning teachers who are new to instructional planning and to establishing developmentally appropriate learning goals with students, and (2) involving students in planning units, learning activities, and assessment instruments.	The curriculum can be created at the classroom, district, and state level. Standards and grade level benchmarks created by the district and/or state communicate mandated requirements (rather than a suggested framework) for teaching and learning in each of the content areas. Students are not involved in instructional planning or creating assessment instruments, but teachers are free to create them, drawing upon the community's cultures and resources to deliver locally relevant, standards-based curriculum.	The curriculum must be developed outside of the classroom at district, state, and national levels. Standards and grade level benchmarks communicate mandated requirements for teaching and learning in each of the content areas. Local funds of knowledge are subordinated to a "what every child must know" approach to curriculum development.

Figure 0.2   Accountability

Radical Progressivism	Moderate Progressivism	Moderate Traditionalism	Radical Traditionalism
Educational accountability has meaning only at the individual, immediate level of classroom practice. Educators, parents, and students are therefore the only legitimate sources of authority for establishing educational goals and defining the means of assessing and evaluating scholastic achievement.	Accountability is oriented to the students, parents, and educators within each school as well as to the broader community served by the school. Value is seen in district-level oversight of the establishment of educational goals and the means of assessing achievement. Educators, parents, students, and leaders at individual school and district levels are recognized as legitimate authors of the public schools' educational goals and accountability efforts.	Accountability is primarily oriented to hierarchical authority at local, state, and federal levels. Authority for defining educational goals and the means for measuring scholastic achievement comes primarily from outside of the classroom, although value is also seen in including educators and parents in the process. Educators, parents, and students are just a few of the "stakeholders" with an interest in assessment data and accountability targets; other stakeholders represent corporate and political interests.	Students and educators must be directly accountable to the government at federal and state levels, and indirectly accountable to the corporate interests that are invested in the schools' production of a capable workforce. Students and educators must be held accountable by governmental agencies for achieving prescribed standards in the interests of stakeholders outside of the classroom, school, and district.

Figure 0.3   Standardization

Radical Progressivism	Moderate Progressivism	Moderate Traditionalism	Radical Traditionalism
The standardization of instructional and assessment practices and resources is not tolerated at any level. Any kind of mandated uniformity imposed on the processes of teaching and learning is counterproductive because of its disregard for the concept of developmental readiness for learning.	Standardizing instructional and assessment practices and resources, while generally undesirable, is occasionally helpful at the school and district levels. When educators are learning to facilitate students' development of particular skills, their decision to adopt and mandate a limited number of student-centered approaches (e.g., 6+1 Trait Writing) is seen as a positive influence on their own growth and professional development.	Having some degree of mandated uniformity of instructional/ assessment practices and resources is essential at school, district, and state levels in order to ensure that all teachers and students are working productively toward achieving district and/or state standards.	Instructional and assessment practices and resources must be standardized to the greatest possible extent to ensure uniformity in the pursuit of achieving mandated standards.

Figure 0.4   Motivation

Radical Progressivism	Moderate Progressivism	Moderate Traditionalism	Radical Traditionalism
Being intrinsically motivated to participate and to do one's best is emphasized as the reason for students, parents, and educators to value school activities. Extrinsic "motivators" (rewards and punishments) are seen as coercions and therefore counter-productive to the ideals of *educere (to draw out; to bring forth)*. Within the paradigm of Radical Progressivism, these coercions are neither justifiable nor appropriate.	While coercive rewards and punishments are seen as counterproductive to the ideals of *educere*, they are also recognized as being occasionally necessary in the process of encouraging students' growth toward a more intrinsic orientation. With the development of intrinsic motivation as the long-term goal (by involving students in the decisions that affect them and by celebrating successes), the use of rewards and punishments is applied in shorter-term contexts.	Extrinsic motivations are emphasized as the reason for educational activities to be valued by students, parents, and educators alike. These include rewards (e.g., good letter grades, class points and parties, merit pay, public recognition for meeting AYP) and sanctions (e.g., poor letter grades, exclusion from class parties, loss of funding, and public disparagement for failing to meet AYP). A Moderate Traditionalist who believes in the value of intrinsic motivation may also believe that extrinsic motivators are effective means for facilitating students' interest in learning.	Extrinsic controls are the only effective way to achieve mandated goals. Students, teachers, and administrators are most effectively managed through the use of rewards and punishments.

Figure 0.5   Classroom and School Environment

Radical Progressivism	Moderate Progressivism	Moderate Traditionalism	Radical Traditionalism
The learning and working environment for students and educators is characterized by a purely democratic governing style: community members' voices are equally valued when important decisions are made (i.e., popular democracy). In this environment, critical thought, respect for individual needs and developmental readiness, courage in asking (and skillfully pursuing) important questions, and cooperation are some of the operative values that are consistently evident.	The learning and working environment is characterized by a governing style in which strong leadership is valued at the classroom, school, and district levels. This paradigm is devoted to democratic and community values (critical thought, individual needs and developmental readiness, asking/pursuing important questions, and cooperation), but ultimate decision-making power lies with classroom, school, and district leadership (similar to the concept of representative democracy). Leaders work with community members at every level to define goals and assess progress.	The learning and working environment for students and educators may be characterized by a top-down management style and values (obedience, uniformity, correctness, and competition). However, moderate traditionalism is also concerned with the more humanistic values of cooperation, respect, and the value of diversity. What distinguishes Moderate Traditionalism from Moderate Progressivism in this realm is that the former's primary goal is to achieve strong control, and the latter's is to achieve strong community.	The learning and working environment in this paradigm is characterized by a top-down management style in which such operative values as obedience, uniformity, correctness, and competition are evident.

Progressive ideas about education are rooted in humanism—that is, in the belief that human beings and their dreams, capacities, and worth must be treated as ends in themselves and not as means for furthering imposed agendas. Vito Perrone captured this idea in summarizing the educational progressivism of John Dewey: "Do we fit the child to the school, or make the school fit the child?" (1991, p. 3). Learner-centered educators are devoted to the idea that schools must work for students rather than the other way around. When schools work for students, young people are respected and challenged to identify and develop their "abilities, interests, ideas, needs, and cultural identities" to the fullest, which can allow their "critical, socially engaged intelligence" to grow in turn. In other words, when schools work for kids, their talents are recognized and developed, facilitating their eventual ability to "understand and participate effectively in the affairs of their community in a collaborative effort to achieve a common good" (John Dewey Project on Progressive Education, 2002, ¶1).

We close this introduction, this orientation to our ideas about progressive thought in education, with a suggestion for new teachers in particular: we urge you to define your world in small enough terms during the first years of your career so that you can, indeed, change it. If you accept this line of thinking, then your job during the initial years of your career is not to challenge the entire system and Change the World. Your job is to work on becoming a great teacher—to change the small world that you, your students, your families, and a few of your colleagues inhabit together. Whether you will eventually have a strong and respected voice in your larger community will depend to a great degree upon whether you are seen as a skilled, caring, and knowledgeable teacher by students, parents, and colleagues in your school. We hope this book might be of use toward that end, as you continue to develop and hone your professional skills and knowledge. Further, we hope that it may encourage educators everywhere to strive to *inspire* every last student whom they serve, and in so doing, to interrupt in small ways every day the reproduction of class-, race-, gender-, and ability-based disparities that limit possibilities for untold millions of children in the United States and around the world.

We launch the coming chapters, inspired ourselves by the words of a fourteen-year-old. In her diary, Anne Frank wrote, "How wonderful it is that nobody need wait a single moment before starting to improve the world." How wonderful, indeed, that we who teach get to know young people whose potential for wisdom, courage, and accomplishment lies in a sense of possibility that we can encourage. There's just no better way to spend a life.

1

Facilitating Community Development in the Classroom

Nathan is an incredibly sweet, volatile, bright, and angry six-year-old who, when eventually tested, will probably be diagnosed with a learning disability and potentially an emotional disorder. He has a very hard time being successful in school and is repeating kindergarten this year without knowing his letters, numbers, or how to interact appropriately with other children. When he is frustrated, he hits other kids and throws powerful tantrums. In his previous kindergarten classroom, another student had perfected the art of goading Nathan into a fit for his own entertainment, in one instance even shouting, "Giddy-up, Nathan! Giddy-up!" His teacher then was in her second year in the classroom; she worked valiantly throughout the year to figure out how to build a sense of community with her students and to reach and teach this troubled little boy. (She was actually not his first kindergarten teacher; Nathan was placed with her in December because his behavior problems proved too challenging in his initial classroom.)

Nathan was placed in Mari's multiage classroom for his second year in kindergarten. Mari is an experienced teacher who continually involves her students in developing and maintaining their classroom community. She has a particular talent for de-escalating potentially volatile situations. Rather than engaging Nathan's masterful tantrums (which had previously been useful in helping him to avoid his difficulties with learning how to do things like read, do math, and make friends), Mari states her expectation, checks to see if Nathan is capable of talking his way toward a solution, and removes his audience *(herself) if he isn't yet able to address the situation cognitively. The confrontations he tries to provoke are simply not engaged; Mari does not see them as threats to her authority so she has no ego investment in "winning" a power struggle with him. She knows that a tantrum with no audience isn't much fun to throw, so she waits at a watchful distance until Nathan can use his words to problem solve. She also finds ways to engage other students in helping him to find his place in the community. With first and second graders in the room who were responsible for developing and maintaining that community in previous years, she has built-in supports for helping Nathan to begin to see himself as a learner.*

During the first week of the new school year, Mari called Nathan's table of students to come read with her and to select their group's new books for that week's "bucket of books." Nathan's three tablemates were girls: two second graders and a first grader, all three confident, tough, independent types who Mari believed could support Nathan and yet not take any grief from him. All three girls were able to read significantly above their own grade level (two had already achieved fourth-grade standards), but when Mari introduced the very simple pattern book she wanted the four students to read with her that day, not one of those girls hesitated for even a moment. They knew the infamous Nathan from the previous year; they knew that he struggled academically and socially. Mari exchanged a knowing look with them and said, "Today I thought we could read The Way I Go to School together." With all seriousness, each girl took turns reading a sentence from that book, even going so far as to think of pointing to each word as they read, modeling their understanding of one-to-one correspondence. "I go to school on a bus." "I go to school in a taxi." And when it was Nathan's turn to read, this little boy who had thus far only shouted "No! I won't!" looked at the pictures and then pointed to each word, saying, "I go to school on a boat."

Mari and the untold thousands of other student-centered teachers in schools around the world are united in a very basic, nonnegotiable belief: classrooms must be good places for all students to be. They know that learning to teach begins with learning how to build a safe, strong, and genuine community with the children in their care. Since Nathan was able to join an already-functioning community of multiage learners, he could be supported from the start of the year not only by his teacher but also by those remarkable classmates who saw on their own how they could help him to belong. They could help him to find his beginning.

Most educators are taught that "classroom management" is one of the essential skills of teaching. We disagree, if only semantically, because this phrase typically, euphemistically refers to the management of human beings rather than of physical environments. When a principal asks a prospective teacher about her classroom management plan, it's understood she is really being asked to describe her behavior management plan, not her classroom. Orderly, respectful behavior is clearly one of the most crucial prerequisites for effective teaching and learning, but how that goal is phrased reveals much about how the relationship between teachers and learners is conceived. Phrasing that goal in terms of having effective classroom management skills is problematic from a student-centered perspective, because from this point of view, *managing* and *educating* children are incompatible processes.

The above may only be a point in semantics, but it's a significant one. The language that we use to describe what we do in the classroom shapes the way we think, just as the way we think determines the language that we use. Educators who set out to *manage* children, according to how that word is defined, approach children with intentions to direct and to handle them; to exert control over them; to make them submissive to the teacher's authority. (These definitions and all that follow were accessed at www.dictionary.com.) From a progressive, humanistic perspective, instruction does not qualify as *education* if a teacher's interactions with his students are aimed at directing, handling, and controlling them. If the teacher's purpose is to make children compliant and submissive, he is more trainer than educator.

As noted in the Introduction, one of the words from which *education* derives is *educere,* a Latin word that means to bring out, to draw forth. This definition for *education* lives in the hearts and minds of student-centered teachers. Because they are concerned with bringing out what children have to offer, with drawing forth the interests and talents and passions and questions that students bring into their classrooms, the progressive educator sees the activities of directing, handling, and controlling children as counterproductive to the processes of teaching and learning. These kinds of activities are, in fact, contradictory to a progressive conception of what it means to be human. Such activities may indeed make children compliant and submissive, but in doing so, they turn schooling away from education and toward indoctrination.

Our interest, then, is in facilitating the skills of community development rather than classroom management. The next chapter actually is devoted to the topic of classroom management, but given the euphemistic nature of that phrase, we use "classroom organization" to describe more aptly the contents of that chapter. Here we will describe what we believe are essential aspects of community development, and we will offer strategies that we have found successful in creating a classroom environment in which every child can feel safe, valued, competent, and powerful.

THE TEACHER'S ESSENTIAL ATTRIBUTES: CONFIDENCE AND HUMILITY, COMPASSION AND FAITH

Teachers who are skilled facilitators of community development believe, first and foremost, in their own authority. This is not the same as being authoritarian. On the contrary, they actively discourage the habit of unquestioning obedience in their students. They do, however, have complete and total confidence in their position as the rightful leader of the class. They are comfortable with their authority, with their leadership status. They do not assume authority; they own it in their bones.

Students of all ages need to know that boundaries exist; to feel safe, they need to know what those boundaries are and that they can be relied upon, and they have a physiological need for safety to be able to learn. (Their neocortex, or their modern, learning brain, cannot physically engage unless their older, reptilian brain detects no threat, no "fight, freeze, or flee" impulse.) Teachers therefore need to be able to provide their students with a classroom environment in which boundaries are clearly, consistently, and calmly applied. Ideally, they involve their students in establishing and maintaining them (more on that in Approach #3 below). The degree of clarity, consistency, and calm that a teacher is able to achieve is directly proportional to the degree of authority she enjoys. Teachers who are unable to be clear, consistent, and calm may be (1) unable to articulate what they value, (2) unwilling to invest the time and the patience that it takes to convince children that those values won't change from day to day, from hour to hour, from minute to minute, and/or (3) unconvinced of their students' ability and/or willingness to respond to an approach that is rooted in respect rather than fear.

It is important to distinguish between presumed and genuine authority. Teachers who presume to have authority simply because they are the teacher (and therefore the students' "superior") face trial by fire every hour of the day because they are engaged in the inherently conflict-ridden project of controlling other human beings. Those who are highly skilled at coercing "desirable" behaviors have orderly classrooms and mostly obedient students, but many of these intellectually and behaviorally docile children are often uninspired and unengaged. According to educator and motivation theorist Spence Rogers (1995, 1998), 75%–80% of schoolchildren are not genuinely motivated by external rewards and punishments like letter grades, suggesting that the great majority of students in traditional, extrinsically oriented classrooms are just putting in their time, either actively or passively resistant to processes of schooling that are done to them.

Control-oriented teachers who are less skilled at manipulating children's behaviors are in a constant power struggle just to keep a semblance of order in their classrooms. This is because their authority comes from assuming a title. Since it comes from a role they happen to be filling rather than from a genuine sense of confidence in who they are and what they have to offer the children in their care, these teachers are essentially acting a part—and students know it. Kids know posers when they see them, and if there is one thing they do not respect, that would be it. Students of all ages do tend to respect and appreciate genuine authority. The question is, what is genuine authority, where does it come from, and how does a beginning teacher who is busy learning so many new things achieve it?

Our thought is that genuine authority comes from a balanced combination of confidence and humility. Confidence comes from a strength of vision and purpose, not from knowing everything there is to know about teaching in every content area, at every level (although deep content knowledge is as essential as the skill of facilitating community development; the intellectual and emotional environments are synergetic). Confidence requires a commitment to professionalism and preparedness that is absolute. Teachers who are comfortable winging it on a daily basis are neither professional nor prepared to teach in a way that honors their students, themselves, or their disciplines. Those who know what they are teaching, why they are teaching it, and how they plan to teach each and every day are professionals who know that confidence begins with: (1) deep knowledge, both of content and methods—which requires a habit of voracious professional reading, a commitment to continual, purposeful reflection, and regular opportunities to discuss and critique classroom practices with colleagues; and (2) consistent, focused instructional planning—with an understanding that while having a plan is essential, being flexible enough to alter or abandon the plan, with good reason, is also necessary. Confidence is an essential component of genuine authority, and the activities described in this paragraph represent specific steps that can be taken to build it.

The other essential component of genuine authority is every bit as important as confidence when it comes to being an effective and respected leader of children, but it is seemingly more difficult to build if it is not already present in a person who has reached adulthood. *Humility* comes from the strength that humor gives and from the knowledge that no person is superior to another. It requires the ability to laugh cheerfully at oneself and to have the strength to be vulnerable. It is a teacher's humility that allows her to wonder with her students; to be reflective about her own practice; to be willing to open herself to the helpful critique of her students, parents, and colleagues; and to be able to offer her own honest critique in return. It is the artful balance of confidence and humility that allows a teacher to lead her students without arrogance and to serve them with authority.

According to education researchers Dick Corbett and Bruce Wilson, urban students consistently name six attributes of good teachers. They are the teachers who "made sure that students did their work, controlled the classroom, were willing to help students whenever and however the students wanted help, explained assignments and content clearly, varied the classroom routine, and took the time to get to know the students and their circumstances" (2002, p. 18). Corbett and Wilson explained that according to students, "their teachers varied tremendously in how well they were able to control students, and the ones who could not maintain control bothered them a lot" (p. 19). One student they interviewed said,

> The kids don't do the work. The teacher is hollering and screaming, "Do your work and sit down!" This makes the ones that want to learn go slower. It makes your grade sink down. It just messes it up for you. The teacher is trying to handle everybody and can't. (p. 19)

Although these researchers and students use the language of behaviorism in describing the good teacher's ability to "control students" and the poor teacher's inability to "handle everybody," they also appeal to the progressive's concern for a student-centered model of authority. While it is clear that students both need and want strong authority figures in their classrooms, it is important to note that the authority they seek is supportive and approachable, not dictatorial and aloof. Appeals for the learner-centered approach of *educere* are revealed in such student comments as: "Kids want teachers who believe in them," "A good teacher takes time out to see if all the kids have what they're talking about and cares about how they're doing," and "They need to have compassion" (Corbett & Wilson, 2002, p. 20). For students to have to appeal for their teachers' faith, concern, and compassion—for these kinds of qualities to even be on kids' radar—is evidence of their having had more than a passing familiarity with what life is like in classrooms where those qualities are absent. From a progressive point of view, any teacher's lack of faith in students and unconcern for their individual well-being is more than singularly tragic. It is an indictment of a system that encourages educators to devote their allegiance to the market values of efficiency and uniformity rather than to the humanistic values described by the John Dewey Project on Progressive Education (2002)—that is, respect for diversity, not unrelenting uniformity, and the importance of critical, socially engaged intelligence.

There is merit in the idea of intentionally ensuring that a teacher's faith in them is "on kids' radar," to help them to understand the role that it plays in the development of a genuine learning community. While a dictionary definition for this kind of faith is "confident belief in the truth, value, or trustworthiness of a person, idea, or thing," our thought is that the elements of hope and imagination must be included when defining the progressive teacher's faith in his students. In this sense, faith is forward-looking. Because the progressive, forward-thinking teacher can see success in every student's future, he is able to help each student to *be* successful. His faith is potent: since he has hope for every child, he can help his students to imagine their own success.

It is the imagination of success that that makes achievement possible. This is one reason why motivation is harder to spark in middle school than in kindergarten. Many thirteen-year-olds have become habituated to having their failures reinforced, and they have lost the ability to imagine themselves as learners—at least in a school setting. The more experience with failure that a student has, the more relevant is Maxine Greene's observation—that "the difficult task for the teacher is to devise situations in which the young will move from the habitual and the ordinary and consciously undertake a search" (1995, p. 24). When a teacher's faith in his students' success is on their radar, they are empowered to reinvent themselves through their teacher's eyes. When they can begin to imagine their own success, they will find the courage to "move from the habitual and the ordinary and consciously undertake a search."

The idea that faith is "confident belief in the truth, value, or trustworthiness of a person, idea, or thing" is problematic in another way: it implies that in the absence of trust, there can be no faith. To our way of thinking, having faith in each and every student's ability to learn and to be a positive, productive member of the community is a basic requirement for all who teach. That faith cannot be conditional. When faith in students is defined as a confident belief in their trustworthiness, however, conditions have been applied. It is now backward- rather than forward-looking, since trust and distrust are learned from the evidence of past experience. We believe that faith and trust are both essential in the development of a classroom community, but not equally so.

Faith is more important, because its forward momentum expands the possibilities we can see in our students—and they in us. All children deserve our faith, but the fact is that not all of them are always trustworthy. They (and we) can do something about that, though; over time, with help, they can teach others that they can be reliable members of the community. Over time, with help, we can teach them that we can be reliable and trustworthy, too.

Imagine the conversations that older students could have in response to open-ended questions about faith and trust! What is the relationship between faith and trust? What do they have to do with the idea of community? Can you build someone's faith in you? Can you build their trust? What must be true for a student to be able to trust her teacher, and vice versa?

To conclude this section on "The Teacher's Essential Attributes," we offer the idea that community development begins with the teacher's disposition toward compassion and faith, confidence and humility. While we will offer specific ideas for accomplishing progressive aims in education in upcoming pages, ideas that we believe will facilitate the growth of confidence, we are unconvinced that strategies exist for achieving compassion, faith, and humility. These, we believe, are essential preconditions for entering the profession. Without them, a person might be able to complete a degree or credential program and to gain employment in a school, but to our way of thinking, that person will not know what it means to be a "real" teacher—one who enjoys genuine authority with her students and who strives to build it in them, in turn.

THE BASIS OF THE TEACHER-STUDENT RELATIONSHIP: MOTIVATION OR COERCION?

Compassion, faith, confidence, and humility are not only the intra- and interpersonal qualities that we believe are required of the truly professional teacher; they are also qualities to appreciate in friends. Friendliness and deeply genuine affection are essential aspects of teacher-student relationships. (We do not believe, however, that being pals with students is an appropriate goal in terms of developing community in the classroom; children need the adults in their lives to provide them with effective models of authority and leadership, and they need their peers to provide camaraderie and friendship.) Students who know beyond doubt that their teacher cares about them can relax into their classroom and into the processes of learning and being together.

Therapists call this prerequisite for affection and relationship "the need for positive regard" (Kristi Sackett, MFT, citing Carl Rogers in personal communication, October 20, 2005). When that need is satisfied, students know that their teacher's approval of them is not conditional; they know that mistakes and failures are not only acceptable and to be expected but also genuinely valued in the learning process. Learning itself is rooted in the student-teacher relationship. The quality of these relationships determines the quality of the emotional environment in the classroom, which in turn determines whether children feel safe enough, valuable enough, and competent enough to risk investing their real selves in learning.

> Most readers will be familiar with the introduction to sex education that typically occurs for fifth graders in the spring, toward the end of the school year. For Carl, a fifth grader with a single mom, having that introduction occur in a strong classroom community allowed him to make personal, social, and academic connections that would not otherwise have been possible. After watching a video on human growth and development with his male classmates, Carl said that he'd been having some dreams lately, "you know, about girls and stuff," and the effects were thoroughly frightening to him. Seeing him painfully red-faced and obviously close to tears, the other boys managed to check their snickering impulse. Several nodded along as Alan reassured Carl that he had those dreams, too, and that his dad had said they were normal. As Carl relaxed, the boys finally let themselves go with the laughter they'd fought to contain. Relieved, Carl was free to find a connection as the final giggles subsided. He brightened visibly with it, saying, "I know we're talking about embarrassing stuff and everything, but this is just like a Socratic discussion. We're just figuring out ourselves!" The quality of the relationships in a classroom determines the quality of the emotional environment, which determines whether kids can feel safe, valuable, and competent enough to risk being real.

An approach to teaching that is rooted in the ideal of *educere* (to draw forth; to bring out) sounds beautiful, but stop a moment and consider the nerve that it takes to let *your* real questions, interests, insecurities, and abilities show—in front of colleagues who may or may not have learned how to be respectful and supportive members of the academic community to which you belong. Clearly, the kind of teaching and learning we are describing takes courage. Therefore, everything having to do with the possibilities of *educere* in your classroom will come down to whether you are able to facilitate trusting, friendly, and fun-loving relationships with your kids—and among them—so that the risk of being real can reside where it's supposed to. That challenge should primarily be undertaken internally, not externally. Students should be able to wrestle with their questions and follow their passions without excessive worry about how others are going to perceive them.

Children take their cues from the adults in their lives when it comes to how they perceive and learn to treat each other. Unfortunately, many of us know teachers who make it clear that in their classrooms, kids can be either winners or losers, successes or failures. Whether such a teacher's obvious or subtle treatment of a particular child is in response to perceptions of that student's academic or physical abilities, personality, willingness to behave as expected, or popularity, the important lesson for every student in the room is that the teacher's approval and affection are conditional. The message they hear is that some students are more worthy than others, and they are encouraged to behave accordingly.

Being accepted and cared for should not be conditional. Healthy relationships are not coercive. The problem this presents for the beginning teacher is that in a society driven by behaviorism (in which "desirable" behaviors are rewarded and "undesirable" ones are punished, an extrinsic control system that many students actively resist), there may appear to be few alternatives to achieving an orderly classroom than to create a management system that is designed to coerce students' obedience. The real problem, though, is that coercing students' obedience through an overt system of rewards and punishments will never, ever result in the establishment of a community of learners who are motivated to be advocates for their own and each other's learning. Coercions do not build relationships and a sense of community. For many students they foster resentment, aggression, and competition.

Fred Rogers, a child development specialist known around the world for the television "neighborhood" he created, embraced the ideal of cooperation rather than competition in helping children to understand the world. Two years before his death in 2003, Mister Rogers told a story to the graduating class of Middlebury College—a story that illustrates the power of conceiving life in larger terms than a competitive, reward-and-punish mind-set is likely to appreciate.

> I wonder if you've heard what happened at the Seattle Special Olympics a few years ago? For the 100-yard dash, there were nine contestants, all of them so-called physically or mentally disabled. All nine of them assembled at the starting line; and, at the sound of the gun they took off—but one little boy stumbled

and fell and hurt his knee and began to cry. The other eight children heard the boy crying. They slowed down, turned around, saw the boy and ran back to him—every one of them ran back to him. One little girl with Down Syndrome bent down and kissed the boy and said, "This will make it better." The little boy got up, and he and the rest of the runners linked their arms together and joyfully walked to the finish line. They all finished the race at the same time. And when they did, everyone in the stadium stood up and clapped and whistled and cheered for a long, long time. People who were there are still telling the story with obvious delight. And you know why? Because deep down we know that what matters in this life is much more than winning for ourselves. What really matters is helping others win, too, even if it means slowing down and changing our course now and then. (Ohanian, 2002, pp. 50–51)

The ultimate question for a teacher seeking to develop community in his classroom is how to help children of every age, from every cultural and socioeconomic background, and from all levels of ability in each area of intelligence to *feel* what those nine kids felt on that track in Seattle. How can we help students to let go of the power games they play—to help them to see social status competitions as obstacles to finding genuine power and authority in their lives? Rather than promoting a coercive, competitive agenda in his classroom, the progressive educator's goal is to help students to find enough personal power and authority (confidence + humility) so that the prospect of helping others can be seen not as a threat to their personal status but as a life-expanding possibility. This goal requires an environment in which students are motivated, not coerced. Students must be continually challenged to be their best selves if they are to have a chance at becoming advocates for their own and others' learning.

For people of all ages to want to do well—to be intrinsically motivated to try hard and to do our best—we must *feel* safe, valued, powerful, and capable (Coopersmith as cited in Brendtro, Brokenleg, & Van Bockern, 2002; Rogers, 1998;). In other words, we must feel a sense of kinship, of relationship, with each other and with the content we are learning. Without this essential emotional attachment, our brains are physically compromised as effective organs for learning (Caine & Caine, 1997; Jensen, 1995, 1998; Kotulak, 1997; Sylwester, 1995; Wolfe, 2001; Zull, 2002). In the absence of these prerequisites for self-esteem and intrinsic motivation, students will resist either passively or actively, either doing just enough to avoid failing grades and behavior that will land them in trouble or deciding not to care about their behavior or schoolwork at all.

Teachers who run their classrooms without concern for the prerequisites of intrinsic motivation rely instead on "extrinsic motivators" or coercions: rewards and punishments designed to promote desirable behaviors and eliminate undesirable ones. These tend to be *highly* effective for achieving short-term compliance, which explains the popularity of behaviorism and the equation of good teaching with strong "classroom management" skills. The problem, of course, is that rewards and punishments emphasize the teacher's power and responsibilities, not the students'. Further, they can discourage the very behaviors and attitudes they are ostensibly designed to promote. Following are some of the findings summarized by Alfie Kohn (1993, 1999) regarding the impact of extrinsic motivators on school performance:

- People who receive an extrinsic motivator for doing something they initially found interesting become less interested in the activity itself and require more and better rewards for subsequently engaging in the activity.
- Extrinsic motivators are very effective in the short term at producing compliance. They are ineffective at making any long-term difference in attitudes and behaviors.
- Extrinsic rewards usually improve performance only at simple tasks.
- Anything presented as a prerequisite for something else comes to be seen as less desirable. As Kohn explained, "'Do this and you'll get that' automatically devalues the 'this'" (1993, p. 76).
- People who participate in an activity where the stakes are raised (i.e., when extrinsic motivators are used) are less creative and do work of poorer quality than do those who participate in an activity for its own sake.
- Intrinsic motivation is eroded not only by the use of rewards. Our internal motivation suffers when we are threatened, watched, forced to work under a deadline, controlled, made to compete against other people, and expect to be evaluated. "In fact," wrote Kohn, "any time we are encouraged to focus on how well we are doing at something—as opposed to concentrating on the process of actually doing it—it is less likely that we will like the activity and keep doing it when given a choice" (1993, p. 80).

Students can be rewarded and punished into compliance but not into a genuine learning community. Community building requires our desire to inspire curiosity, creativity, critical thought, and cooperation, which is a more difficult undertaking than coercing obedience. It's easier to be a dictator than a democrat, though; easier to aim for mere compliance. It is easier, for some, to tell Sara that she isn't invited to the class party because she didn't do her homework or because she misbehaved once too often, than to figure out how to honor her reality and her need to belong. It wouldn't occur to the progressive educator, whose emphasis is on building a trusting and respectful relationship with Sara, to create intentionally a social context that has a good chance of excluding her (like the class party that was planned with conditions for inclusion in mind). The learner-centered teacher wants all of her students to know that they always belong in the community.

This doesn't mean that students can never be excluded from an activity. A student who does not behave respectfully and safely toward others certainly requires the consequence of temporarily losing the privilege of being near other children. But a learner-centered approach to this child is focused always on helping her to understand that she is the person who is in charge of her inclusion as well as her exclusion from classroom activities; there is no predetermined plan for identifying who will and will not be invited to participate. The assumption of belonging requires that each student be given opportunities to demonstrate the ability to be a productive member of the community, and when a child fails in this, the assumption of belonging requires that she has chances to correct her behaviors and to fix the problems she has created. Belonging is as much about responsibility as it is about the right to be included.

WHO DECIDES WHO BELONGS?
A NOTE ON INCLUSIVE EDUCATION

The federal government did a good thing in the 1970s by mandating that children with special learning needs have a right to a free and appropriate education, which, by law, must take place in a classroom environment that is least restrictive for them. It did damage at the dawn of the twenty-first century by powerfully reinforcing through federal law (i.e., "No Child Left Behind," the 2001 reauthorization of the Elementary and Secondary Education Act of 1965) the idea that children should develop at the same pace toward the same goals. By defining success in terms of the achievement of uniform standards on a mandated time line, the developmentally illogical goal for every child to be "on grade level" is reinforced.

Among other damaging effects, this kind of thinking effectively distances children with special needs from their rightful place in least-restrictive classrooms with their peers. By placing a premium on standard rather than individual development, the fundamental need and right of every child to belong is violated. With the weight of federal law pressing down from above, teachers are encouraged to exclude students with special needs from least-restrictive placements in general education classrooms and to focus their attentions on the students who really "count." This reality is illustrated by the following observation by a Texas teacher who said,

> Ana's got a 25 percent. What's the point in trying to get her to grade level? It would take two years to get her to pass the test, so there's really no hope for her. I feel like we might as well focus on the ones there's hope for. (Booher-Jennings, 2006a, ¶6)

"Educational triage" is the phrase that sociologist Jennifer Booher-Jennings used to describe this unfortunate, if predictable, response to the mandated uniformity of educational expectations and outcomes, explaining that "when a low-performing student enters a teacher's classroom, he or she is seen as a liability rather than as an opportunity to promote individual student growth" (2006b, Educational Triage section, ¶10). If schools and classrooms were allowed to develop with the ideals of *educere* in mind, teachers would be encouraged to see students as they are, rather than how they are supposed to be. Students would be challenged at their own developmental levels, rather than at the mandated level that has been prescribed as normal for their age. A progressive classroom provides such sanctuary for all of its students, all of whom come with needs that are unique to them.

Two years ago, Caroline requested that an incoming kindergartner with Down Syndrome be placed in her classroom. Although she has no formal certification in special education, Nick's parents were enthusiastic about the idea. They ignored the strong misgivings of the site specialist from his previous school, who doubted that this five-year-old boy could be successful with a teacher who is certified in general rather than special education. Nick is now in his second year in Caroline's class; his parents retained him to give him another year in a classroom where he is seen in terms of his abilities. Caroline is consistent in her determination to ensure a deep sense of belonging in Nick, as with all of her students.

One day during his second year in the class, Nick raced into the room before the morning bell had rung, breathless with excitement. While tearing to get his backpack off, he explained to Caroline, "Cards! Cards! Backpack! Cards!" Knowing that his sixth birthday was approaching, she said, "Oh wow, Nick, do you have some birthday invitations in your backpack?" He smiled and nodded in reply, beaming with the joy of it all. After Caroline helped him off with his backpack, he hurried to take out the invitations. Then he showed her each one in turn, exclaiming, "Yes! Birthday party. A party! And Sam will come, and Melinda will come, and Abe will come . . . All the families will come." His eyes, and Caroline's too, were swimming in tears by the time he concluded, with his arms outstretched and hands open skyward, "And I be so happy!"

Our social and cultural compulsion for fitting children to schools tends to discourage some children's access to regular, daily life with their peers. Sometimes teacher education programs compound the problem. By treating the preparation of special education and general education teachers as entirely separate processes, a certain attitude about the education of "those children" is encouraged throughout the profession. Special educators are attributed with having skills and knowledge that are beyond those of the teachers of "typical" children. While it is true that teachers with formal backgrounds in serving children with disabilities may be more thoroughly prepared to address their unique learning needs, it is not therefore true that general educators inherently lack the skills and knowledge for teaching children with special needs. General and special educators, working together to support the needs of all children, have the power to ensure that every child gets to know that they belong in our classrooms.

FROM THEORY TO PRACTICE: STRATEGIES FOR FACILITATING RELATIONSHIP AND COMMUNITY

Approach #1: Be real.

Speak with your students in the same tone that you use to speak with adults, demonstrating your respect for their humanity. Talk with them, not down to them. Referring to yourself in the third person, as many teachers of young children seem to do, is simply odd. If you are unsure of this, try it out with children you don't know in another context—in the park, in the library, or in line at the movies—and watch for their reactions. Check out their parents' reactions, too.

Model the idea that no person is superior to another by treating your students as human beings who are every bit as deserving of respect as you are. This does not mean that you must invite students to call you by your first name, although we believe doing so is perfectly fine. In particularly conservative communities, however, some parents may consider the use of your first name overly familiar. Ultimately, your decision about how to have your students address you is a matter of your own comfort level and your perception of community norms. The real issue is whether or not your students respect you, making the form of address a secondary issue.

Have a sense of humor, and encourage it in your kids. Be real with your emotions. If you are angry or sad, it's okay to show it as long as you don't try to make students accept responsibility for how you're feeling. You can help them learn how to express their feelings appropriately and responsibly by modeling productive ownership of your own emotions. (Compare: "Why can't you just be quiet and do your work? I'm so *tired* of having to ask you again and again!" to "I'm feeling *really* frustrated right now. Help me to figure out what's going on. How can we work better together?") Resist the temptation to be pals with your students; they have enough friends. If they don't, they need your help to learn how to make friends their own age. They need you to be their leader—a leader who is friendly, approachable, consistent yet reasonably flexible, and confident. In respecting you, they will be learning how to respect themselves and each other.

Finally, work to overcome the socialization you have probably experienced, as most of us have, that encourages a false response to people who are somehow different from dominant norms. Many of us were taught by our parents that it's not polite to stare at a man wearing a turban or at a woman in a wheelchair. While they were right, an unintended, destructive message was also delivered: there's something wrong with people who are different from us, so they're sort of embarrassing to be around. Consequently, many of us learned to pretend not to see difference.

Many teachers voice this well-intentioned but misguided sentiment when they say that they don't even notice what color their students are, that they're all just beautiful little people to them. The fact is that we all *do* notice visibly apparent differences if we have the gift of sight. Pretending otherwise is disrespectful, since "not noticing" this aspect of our students' identities is to erase a defining element of who they are. This tendency to homogenize children contributes to a classroom culture in which "normalcy" (i.e., uniformity) is every child's most urgent goal. Sapon-Shevin perfectly captured the progressive educator's need to be real when it comes to acknowledging and respecting differences. "The goal must not be 'not noticing,'" she cautioned. "The goal should be to notice, understand, respond, and connect" (1999, p. 64). While her focus was on creating inclusive classrooms for children with special needs, her words are equally relevant when applied to the many other kinds of diversity that our students embody:

> One sometimes hears it said that the "successful" inclusive classroom is one in which "you can't tell the kids with disabilities apart from the regular kids." While the underlying sense of equity and fair treatment reflected in that statement is admirable, the goal itself is often unattainable and probably undesirable, as well. Some of the children "included" in typical classrooms have differences that are quite noticeable, and no amount of community building or successful accommodation will mask their unique characteristics. Setting a goal of "invisibility" for children with disabilities does not help us think well about how children's differences are responded to or how they are incorporated into the daily life and activities of a classroom. Encouraging Rowena to hide her hearing aids behind her hair so that no one sees them will not help other students learn how to communicate with a classmate with a hearing loss. It also communicates to Rowena that wearing hearing aids is somehow bad or shameful. The goal of the inclusive classroom is that all students feel that they belong and are able to contribute to the class. (p. 65)

Approach #2: Create class norms together.

Note: Our ideas about the importance of engaging students in establishing and maintaining norms are shaped by the work of the National School Reform Faculty (NSRF), of which we are members. The NSRF is "a professional development initiative that focuses on developing collegial relationships, encouraging reflective practice, and rethinking leadership in restructuring schools—all in support of increased student achievement" (National School Reform Faculty, n.d.).

Rather than honoring only your values and expectations for behavior, involve your students in the process of creating class norms. This will require your trust in their need to be in an environment that is under control and in their desire to demonstrate their knowledge of right and wrong in positive ways. You can begin the process of creating class norms for behavior that everyone will agree to honor in this way: Ask your students to think about what they need from you and from each other so they can do their best. Tell them that as a class, you're going to brainstorm two lists, two sets of norms or expectations: one for you and another one that will apply to everyone in the room.

First make the list of process norms, or students' ideas about what they need from you. By starting with an invitation for students to think and talk about what they need from you, you will be demonstrating your comfort with your own authority, exercising that balanced combination of confidence and humility described earlier. You will be modeling the idea that true strength requires a willingness to be vulnerable. At the same time, though, your leadership in this must be definite. Don't laugh along with or pretend you don't hear disrespectful comments or mean-spirited "jokes" that are at your expense or anyone else's. Your students need to see that it will be safe to be vulnerable. By demonstrating recognition of your students' right to have high expectations of you, you will be creating a mind-set of fairness, preparing them for the idea that every class member, including you, has the right to have high expectations of them.

Start by asking your students to think about what they need from you to be able to enjoy your class and to do their best. Give older students two to three minutes to write at least three ideas, completing the sentence, "For me to be able to do my best and to enjoy this class, I need my teacher to . . ." Then ask students to share their ideas, recording each one on a large sheet of chart paper. Go around the room, giving each student a chance to add to the list. After everyone has had a turn and all ideas have been shared, take time to talk through any proposed norms with which you or any students have a problem, explaining objections and proposing revised ideas or language. Then ask the class to look at the list to see if any ideas can be combined or categorized under common headings. Tell students that you will take the list, organize it, and provide each student with a copy the next day. Make a poster of it, too, to hang on the wall—or ask students to come up with a way to communicate and illustrate these ideals for your behavior.

When you do distribute copies of these "process norms" the next day, ask students to double-check the accuracy of that initial draft. Provide a few minutes for their review, demonstrating your commitment to their ongoing authorship and ownership of the process. Your goal in all of this is emphatically *not* to get student "buy-in." Leaders seek buy-in when they have already made all of the important decisions and all they want is compliance. In seeing your students as subjects, not objects, your goal is bigger and more respectful, more concerned with their agency than their obedience.

After students have had a chance to talk about what they need from you, ask them to think about what they need from themselves and from each other to be able to do their best and to enjoy the class. For younger students, doing this in a separate session, either later in the day or the next day, is a good idea. Come up with a list of "community norms" by first having each student come up with two or three ideas to complete the sentence, "For me to be able to do my best and to enjoy this class, every member of our group must . . ." Follow the same procedure as before, allowing kids time to think about what they need and then to share their ideas. (This is a good process to follow whenever you ask your students to engage in a brainstorming session. Always give them time to think alone, first, before sharing ideas with the group. This offers *all* students a better chance for active participation, rather than encouraging the verbal extroverts to dominate.) You should feel welcome to add your own ideas, too. As a member of the classroom community, your needs are also important.

A particular community norm that is a good idea to include, if students don't come up with it, is that every person has the right to "pass" if they want to, whenever public sharing of ideas is requested. By including the right to pass in your community norms, you will be facilitating students' comfort level in your classroom by showing them that they have a choice, that they are in control of what they want to share. Furthermore, most kids want to participate actively if the activity is worthwhile. By explicitly allowing them the power to pass, you'll be implicitly sending the message that superficial participation isn't what you're after. You'll be promoting genuine engagement in the long run.

After all ideas have been recorded, ask the students if there is anything on the list that is giving them trouble, any expectation that they might not be able to live up to. Allow time for students to revise the wording of any troublesome norms, making sure to check with the whole group on whether compromises are acceptable to the whole. Do not allow a norm to stand that any student refuses to honor. Let it be the students' problem to find a way to resolve disagreements and to reach acceptable compromises. When categories for the norms have been suggested and a draft is complete, tell students you will type them and provide everyone with a copy for them to review the next day. Make a poster, too, or give students time to make their own. Again, allow time for their review of that initial draft when they get it.

While you are brainstorming community norms, if you have students who are actively sabotaging the process and refusing to agree to one or more of the proposed norms, keep yourself focused on being clear, consistent, and calm. Resist the urge to take responsibility for the problem by imposing your own solution. Instead, engage the group in naming the problem (not naming the people who are creating the problem), defining and clarifying it, and proposing solutions (see Approach #5 on class meetings below). Do not resort to threatening a student who is sabotaging the norm-writing process with calling his parents or the principal, because the message sent is that parents and administrators are your enforcers. This approach undermines your own authority, and it divides the community by making outsiders of parents and administrators. Instead, work with individual students and with the class as a whole on the skills of naming, defining, clarifying, and solving problems together. Save referrals to parents and principals for problems that involve student safety or that have proved over time to be beyond your ability to negotiate.

If this approach sounds overly naïve or utopian, it is because we live in a society in which interactions between adults and children are so consistently defined in terms of coercion and control rather than respect and cooperation. This means that in some contexts, your faith in students will need to be demonstrated more patiently and determinedly than in others. It does not mean that the ideals of *educere* are appropriate only for some children. However, it will always and forever mean that you will need to match your faith in your students with your intelligence and creativity. Kids will surely play you if you let them, so the faith we're describing isn't simplistic and blindly trusting. It's up to you to provide a structured system in which students are not only invited and challenged to be their best selves but also supported and held accountable for their behavior in the process. Effective approaches for guiding a student's behavior will, over time, move the locus of control for accountability from you to the student. On the other hand, you'll know an approach is ineffective if (1) you keep using it and the behavior hasn't changed and (2) you continue to be more responsible than the student for monitoring behavior as time goes by.

If you find yourself policing accountability to your community norms with any individual student or group of students over time, you need to alter your strategies. You'll know it's time to consider changing your approach if you feel distinctly uneasy and unsatisfied with how something is going in the classroom. Learn to pay attention to that uneasy feeling and to trust that it's there for good reason. When you are uneasy, focus hard on the feeling and give yourself time to figure out what is causing it. The first step in solving any problem is to name it, and that is what this feeling of discomfort is telling you that you need to do. Only when you can name the problem and describe it can you share responsibility with your students for solving it. Call a special class meeting (see Approach #5 below) if you need to, describe the problem you're seeing, and enlist your students' help.

Close the norm-writing session by debriefing it. Ask students what the process of writing norms together did for them, or failed to do for them. Specifically inviting kids to talk about what *didn't* work requires your willingness to be vulnerable. Asking for both positive and negative feedback also builds trust in you and in the process. Encourage them to talk through their ideas about why you chose to spend valuable class time on such an activity. This is a good opportunity to think with your students about the idea that spending time up front can save time and energy in the long run, since your goal is not to police students' behavior but to facilitate their own sense of freedom and responsibility, their power and self-control.

Emphasize the idea that these two sets of norms represent your collective ideals. Assure students that there will be times when you and they are unable to live up to them, but that they represent the group's highest hopes. Do not laminate the posters that you make of these norms—and tell your kids that you won't be treating them like a finished product—because you expect that they will change and grow along with the class. Tell students that you will be periodically asking them to review the norms so that everyone can see whether you all are living up to the class's valued ideals. Review them at least once a week at the beginning of the year (a suggested procedure is described in Approach #3), then once every three or four weeks after you and your students have established a sense of familiarity and confidence in them. Do not succumb to the temptation to refer to the norms only when students are breaking them. Doing so strips these agreements of their power to build community, because then they simply become a mechanism of control, a tool that you use for bopping students over the head when they fail. Worthwhile ideals are hard to realize. They require our patience and our faith in children, as well as in ourselves.

A final note to keep in mind when it comes to the establishment of norms for any ongoing group, for people of every age, is that norms *will* be made whether or not the group's formal leader takes charge of the process. If the process of establishing norms is not done explicitly under the guidance of a strong facilitator, group norms will still exist. It's just that they will be created informally by the most powerful members of the class, and they will be the unspoken, unwritten rules by which the group operates. Inviting every member of any group to participate in creating expectations serves to bring norms for behavior into the open, to put them right out on top of the table as a legitimate topic of concern and discussion. This overt process protects the right of every group member to have a voice in the process of defining his or her experience.

Approach #3: Don't stop when norms are named. Now teach your students how to take responsibility for them and to make them real.

Students tend to be very well accustomed to the way that school rules and behavioral expectations are supposed to work. Once those expectations are established, with or without students' participation, adults are supposed to be responsible for ensuring that children's behaviors conform to them. Many administrators, teachers, and parents share this view. From a learner-centered perspective, however, this way of thinking encourages a thoroughly false sense of community. Clearly, educators are responsible for providing firm guidance, for ensuring that students are safe, and for intervening when a particular child or group of children isn't willing or able to meet established behavioral expectations. But from a learner-centered perspective, the ultimate goal must always be to help children move closer—in whatever-sized steps they are capable of taking—to being responsible for their own behavior and learning. Therefore establishing norms with students is only the first step. They become real when students own them through regular and ongoing opportunities to review, revise, and maintain them.

When you review the norms, first ask your students to look at the process norms, the ideals they hold for you. Ask them to meet with one or two other students and to agree on at least one thing that they think you're doing really well and one thing that they wish you would focus on a bit more. Assure students that nothing they say will affect their grade and nothing they say will affect your relationship with them (but only if you're confident that this will be true, that you have the ability to hear the feedback you request). Allow a few minutes for this conversation and then ask for public feedback. Make notations next to the expectations that the students identify as your strengths and weaknesses, reminding them that not everyone has to agree with any small group's or individual's opinion. This is an opportunity for discussion and critique, and the opinions that people offer are intended simply to provoke conversation for the purpose of helping you to grow closer toward realizing those ideals. Tell students up front that you expect them to be able to identify areas in which you need to grow; if they have to legitimately struggle to find a growth area for you, celebrate the opportunity with them to revise the process norms to include more sophisticated expectations. Take time to talk publicly through your response to students' feedback. Provide opportunity for the norms to be revised as needed.

Then give the same small groups a few minutes to look at the expectations they named for themselves. Ask them to try to find at least one thing that they are each doing very well and one thing they could improve. It's a good idea at the beginning to invite students to comment only on how they themselves are performing relative to the class norms. Inviting them to comment on how the entire class is doing can be a divisive thing, especially at the beginning of the year before trust and respect may be established. Toward the end of the year, you might ask students to make observations about how the class as a whole is doing.

Again, ask for public sharing. Remind students that one individual's or group's opinion does not make anything true for the whole class. Prepare students for this conversation by talking about why you are having them identify things that individual students are doing well and not so well, rather than initially inviting students to make observations about the whole class. Tell them that eventually, the goal is for members of the class to be able to discuss how the group is doing as a whole without causing or taking offense. Offer time for students to talk through the thoughts they heard from each other, to set goals for improvement, and to record and explain those goals in writing. Finally, ask students if they think any norms need to be added, removed, or revised.

Close the norm review session by debriefing it. Say something like, "Okay, now step back from the content of this conversation and think about the process we just went through together. What did it do for you, or fail to do for you, to have a chance to think and talk about how we're doing in terms of the expectations we established for ourselves?" Giving students a chance to reflect honestly on an activity not only builds their sense of ownership and control over their experience in school, it also establishes you as a person who cares about students' opinions. It humanizes you and the students in equal measure. This kind of debriefing process is often an excellent approach to use after academic lessons, too. When we have students do activities but don't give them time to process their experience, they tend to be able to recall what they did but not what they learned. Giving students time to think about *why* they did an activity helps to clarify and to seat the learning.

Students of every age are capable of creating and maintaining class norms. Furthermore, in our experience, students of every age (adults, too) appreciate opportunities to have a say—that is, to have power—in defining their learning and working environments. However, it is difficult to engage some students in the processes of maintaining and honoring norms. These uncooperative few are typically students who have learned that adults are not trustworthy, that the system is not about them, and that the only power they will have in school is what they can take for themselves. They may have spent too many years in classrooms in which "good" behavior was coerced, having learned that the only reasons for them to cooperate were to get good grades or the teacher's approval or class points for a party on Friday afternoon. If they don't care about their grades, adult approval, or a chance to eat ice cream and pizza during school, the coercive teacher's leverage is gone, and all he can do then is to think up ever more punitive consequences in order to force the student to "care."

The problem for the student-centered teacher who is trying to establish genuine opportunities for children to have power and voice in their classrooms is that these students have learned not to trust. They have learned to resist. They have eliminated the possibility of failure by not trying to succeed in the first place: they've perfected the fine art of "not-learning" (Kohl, 1994, p. 2). With these children, your particular challenge is to earn trust, not to force compliance. With extremely defiant students, there are simply no easy solutions. Working consistently with them every day to build in small ways their sense of safety, value, competence, and autonomy is all you can do.

An approach you can use to gain cooperation from moderately resistant students or entire classes is to create a self-assessment form based on the class norms. Have students complete that self-assessment daily or weekly at the beginning of the year (less often as the need diminishes) and use these assessments of their behavior as the basis for individual goal-setting and problem-solving conferences between you and that student. Eventually asking parents and/or your principal to participate in these conferences may be necessary for especially resistant kids—but try to facilitate this kind of conference as a genuine conversation in which you, the student, the parent, and/or principal work together to (1) identify the areas in need of improvement, (2) choose the most important one on which to focus at first, and (3) set a date for a follow-up meeting to recognize progress. At the follow-up meeting, hopefully a new goal will be set, if another is necessary. If progress on the first goal wasn't evident, however, the group will create a plan together that specifies consequences if the student continues to disregard community norms.

Norms can evolve through the process of routine review, potentially becoming more sophisticated as the year goes by. For example, a realistic goal at the beginning of the year may be for every class member to "Listen carefully when others are speaking," but if students agree in February that this norm is consistently honored, they can look for new ways to push themselves in this area. The need to listen carefully remains, but that basic requirement for effective communication will be implied in the more challenging goal of "Ask speakers productive questions." Part of the challenge, part of the fun, is to help students to think through what *productive* means in this context and then to facilitate their skills in posing great questions of each other, as well as of you. The ongoing review and critique of this particular norm can help you to help your students understand a very powerful idea: that the people who share responsibility for the questions are the ones who enjoy true ownership of the learning.

Approach #4: Cultivate a calm and patient manner while upholding class norms and other clearly stated expectations.

Consistency is the defining element of the "tipping point" when it comes to developing a genuine sense of community with the learners in your care. Your goal is to do all that you can to ensure that behaviors in your classroom "tip" in a direction that will promote the development of a safe and strong learning community for every member of your class.

Malcolm Gladwell (2002) described the concept of the tipping point as that moment when a critical mass has been reached and a change in group behavior results. In other words, if you were to observe a single incident of a certain behavior, whether it's positive or negative, your own behavior would be unlikely to change as a result. But if many people around you were engaging in that same behavior, you would be far more likely to engage in it yourself. One stranger who smiles and holds the door for you, for example, may not affect your decision to smile and hold the door for the person behind you; but if many people around you were being friendly and helpful to others, you would be more likely to be friendly and helpful yourself. If one car were to zoom by at 90 miles per hour when you and everyone else were following the 65-mile-an-hour speed limit, you probably wouldn't decide to speed up; but if almost everyone around you were speeding, it's more likely that you would, too. The tipping point in both cases is where enough people are engaging in a behavior to influence others' choices.

Making sure that students' behaviors are more likely to tip toward the goal of community development rather than away from it depends greatly on how clear, calm, and consistent you can be every minute of every day.

Every new teacher can repeat the mantra—that it's important to be consistent—but not every teacher understands *why* that consistency is important or *how* to achieve it all of the time. The first question, why consistency is important, may seem obvious. If a teacher isn't consistent, she will "lose control" of her classroom. But the previous discussion of the tipping point invites a deeper and more student-centered understanding of the problem. A student-centered, humanistic perspective on guiding children's behavior is informed by the basic belief that while human beings resist being controlled, they want to be in an environment that feels safe and "under control." In other words, students want to tip toward the common good that they have helped to define through their class norms, but that desire will be kept alive only in an environment in which those norms are fairly and consistently applied to every member of the group.

Although Gladwell did not specifically address how important it is for teachers to be consistent if their goal is to develop safe and strong classroom communities, his explanation of the tipping point perfectly illustrated that idea. He described a classic example of the effects on a neighborhood when a broken window is not repaired. That broken window sends a message of neglect, signaling a breakdown in the social norms of care and attention. Left unattended, one "broken window"—or violated norm—encourages the spread of social breakdown; as more windows are broken, destruction, violence, and other anticommunity behaviors become increasingly acceptable. That one broken window serves as the impetus for moving, or tipping, the culture of the neighborhood away from the values of mutual respect and concern, just as the one time that a teacher doesn't follow through on reinforcing appropriate expectations serves as the impetus for moving the culture of the classroom away from cooperation and mutual advocacy. Relentless consistency in upholding commonly held social values (i.e., classroom norms) is required for building strong communities in which every member feels safe and valued.

In short, as quickly as many adults will break the speed limit if they think they can get away with it, many kids will be equally quick to tip away from community ideals as soon as they see that those ideals don't always count or that they don't apply to everyone. People of all ages need to be helped to be their best selves and to make community-building choices. The importance of consistency, then, isn't about a teacher's ability to maintain control; it's about how determined he is to ensure that students have opportunities to be in control of themselves. It's about helping them to be their best selves so that they can live up to their community's ideals.

That said, it's a lovely sentiment without meaning—unless the "how" of consistency is also addressed. Students need opportunities to learn how to be in control of themselves and to make community-building choices, but it's a sure bet that they're going to make mistakes along the way. Part of the help that they need is in being able to see those mistakes as opportunities to learn. If every member of the group is to have a chance at feeling safe and valued in your classroom, students need to see that appropriate and logical consequences will *always* result when they make choices that are hurtful to others and damaging to the learning community.

It is important to note, however, that what is appropriate and logical for one student may not be so for another! The idea of relentless consistency in this context refers to the need for your unflagging determination to uphold class norms and your own high expectations; it does not mean that your responses to different students who fall short of honoring a particular expectation must be identical. In a classroom where diversity is truly valued, you and your students will be able to see that different needs are logically accommodated in different ways.

Therefore, while the "why" of consistency is answered in the argument of the tipping point, the "how" of it is answered with appropriate and logical consequences. There's a good chance, for example, that if no consequence were attached to the act of breaking the speed limit, many of us would probably exceed it more often than not—even though we understand that driving slowly is safer, more fuel efficient, and therefore better for everyone's well-being and the environment. Fines and the threat of losing the license to drive are necessary consequences for helping many of us to behave in community-building ways when we're on the road. The consistency-oriented challenge for teachers who are devoted to the ideal of a classroom community, then, is to figure out how to apply consequences for breaking class norms in such a way as to help students *want* to follow the rules and improve their behavior. In working toward this goal, teachers must recognize and exercise their powers of discretion—differentiating their responses to students (an intervention may be highly effective for one student but not for another) but not their commitment to upholding those norms. The trick is to ensure that the end result of the intervention is more encouraging than discouraging for students who are still learning how to behave well.

The more traditional orientation to "classroom management" requires the teacher to be in control of students and to manage their behaviors for them. This is often an extremely effective approach to improving students' behavior—as long as the teacher is nearby. If your goal is larger than classroom management, though—if it is to help students to be in control of themselves and of their environment by allowing them to manage their own conduct—then relentless consistency in providing appropriate and logical consequences for anticommunity behaviors will be key to your students' success.

Entire books are written on this crucial topic of how to guide students' behavior effectively and respectfully (e.g., Glasser, 1998a; McEwan, 2000; Nelson, Lott, & Glenn, 2000; Strachota, 1996; Weinstein & Mignano, 2007). Because we believe that positive relationships and safe, strong communities are among the most important prerequisites for effective teaching and learning in schools, we strongly urge you to read and discuss such books with other teachers and parents and to have conversations with your students about the ideas that resonate with you. Following are a few of the ideas that we believe are important guidelines for responding to students whose behaviors undermine the learning community.

(1) Approach the student with the goal of understanding the problem (and of helping the student to understand it, too) rather than simply of stopping it. Certainly, you want inappropriate behavior to stop, but if you also want the child to be in control of himself in that environment, he needs to know that you care about him enough to be fair in addressing the problem. Students are more likely to "behave" in classrooms that are led by teachers who are fair. These teachers, because they obviously care about every child and genuinely want to understand what students are going through, are typically successful at de-escalating tough situations and giving students opportunities to fix the problems that their negative behaviors have caused. They are good at "turning down the heat" as Tarry Lindquist (2002) put it:

> Every time I notice that I feel like yelling at the kids, or wringing my hands and pleading with them, I find I've inadvertently turned up the heat. I have (1) required too much (2) in too little time and/or (3) given too few or too many directions (4) with too little background or (5) insufficient resources. Obviously,

I need to "turn down the heat" by changing or reshaping the activity. (p. 57)

On the other hand, teachers whose interventions are punitive from the start tend to have an escalating effect on some students' negative behaviors. You'll know that you're an escalator of disruptive behavior if you find that your interventions tend to make students more aggressive and problematic rather than less so. If your goal is simply to stop disruptive behavior, and if you are more likely to make assumptions about students than to try to understand their actions—that is, if you are trying to establish control instead of community—you may soon find that you're one of those teachers whose more challenging kids tend to spend a lot of time in the hallway or in the office. It happens. If it has happened to you, it's all right. It's reversible. It just takes patience, consistency, confidence in yourself, faith in your students, and an understanding that some kids need to work as hard or harder at learning how to control their own behavior as they do at learning academic content and skills. Turning things around also requires your compassion and your instructional creativity, since a great many students need to act out behaviorally because they don't know how to be successful academically and/or socially.

Approaching students' behavior problems with the mind-set of understanding them sends a powerful and simple message: you care. Kids who have their own reasons for knowing that you care about them will come to realize, too, that the consequences that are sure to follow their poor choices are necessary *because* you care about them and because you want to help them to belong. Why else would you go to the trouble of being so tenaciously clear, calm, and consistent with them?

(2) Consequences need to make sense to students if they are to learn from them. The consequences that make the most sense are the ones that give kids a chance to fix the problems that their behaviors have caused. Put another way, the problem holds the solution. If a student's behavior hasn't caused a genuine problem for herself or for anyone else in the room, you will be hard pressed to identify an appropriate and logical consequence for it. The implication here is that not all "bad" behaviors require an overt consequence. In the overwhelming majority of cases, in fact, students are willing and able to correct their own behavior when you simply show them that you *see* them—which goes a long way toward communicating that you care about them. While new teachers are typically taught that "planned ignoring" is a useful strategy for

dealing with minor misbehaviors, this approach can backfire. Many students will be swift to tip away from community norms if they are allowed to believe that you are unaware of what's happening. Using "the look" to communicate anything from amused awareness to rapidly diminishing patience allows the student to understand that you see her and that you have faith in her ability to correct the behavior on her own.

When an overt consequence is necessary because a student's behavior is genuinely problematic for herself and/or others, you can help her to name and to understand the real difficulties that she is causing; she will then be more able to participate intelligently in determining an appropriate consequence with you. More important, if she feels encouraged in the process of learning to behave well because her mistakes and bad decisions are consistently used as learning opportunities, she's more likely to make better choices in the future. Class meetings provide an excellent forum for teaching students how to name and describe real problems and identify their possible solutions.

A final note about consequences: address them when the need arises. As McEwan noted, when we emphasize consequences before a problem even exists, we are essentially underscoring our expectation of failure (2000, p. 32).

(3) The need for "relentless consistency" on your part does not imply that you need to be rigid in your expectations. You and your students have the right to change your minds about how things should be done in your classroom. You just can't change them every day. Flexibility is a good thing when changes are made thoughtfully and for sound, clear reasons; but if students know that your willingness to follow through on expectations can change from day to day or from minute to minute, they'll make you pay for your unreliability by testing you from day to day and from minute to minute, right up to the end of the school year. The reason for this is simple: figuring out adults' boundaries is every kid's job, and some students can make a school career out of that specialization. Anyone who has ever noticed how differently these particular students will behave depending upon which adult is working with them knows the role that clear and consistent boundaries play in children's lives.

Teachers whose boundaries shift constantly will be constantly tested, which naturally introduces an element of antagonism to the student-teacher relationship. Just as naturally, these teachers will be unnecessarily exhausted at the end of every day. More important, though, constant testing of boundaries means that responsibility for students' behavior and for the classroom environment can never be shifted to where it belongs. Students who are trying to figure out how far they can bend the rules at any given moment don't have the opportunity or the confidence they need to internalize the value of those rules in their own lives. They need us for that.

Relentless consistency for the first month of the school year will teach your students that you are reliable, and they can relax into the confidence that predictability brings. You will need to continue to be consistent throughout the year, of course, but by focusing particularly hard on building that sense of predictability during the first month, you will establish a climate in your classroom that your students can count on and can internalize over time. The importance of your consistency will not diminish, but the day-to-day, minute-by-minute need for it will, as your students learn to accept more and more responsibility for themselves. The fruit of your consistency in reinforcing agreed-upon norms and expectations will be your students' realization that "that's just the way we do things here." With this realization, they will have both the opportunity and the confidence to shift some of the behavior-monitoring responsibility from you to them, to where it belongs.

Approach #5: Hold weekly class meetings.

In 1996, Bob Strachota wrote a highly readable book, *On Their Side: Helping Children Take Charge of Their Learning*, an excellent orientation for teachers whose goal is to develop classroom community rather than to control and manage their students' behavior. In it, he shared his discovery, after many years in the classroom, that students learn best when they have genuine opportunities to take responsibility for solving their own classroom problems. The failures he experienced in the first years of his career, failures that came from imposing his solutions for students' problems, are agonizingly familiar to those of us who spent our early years struggling our way from a mind-set of behaviorism to one of constructivism in our teaching. The reality that Strachota discovered is that no problem can be truly solved unless the people who own it get to work their own way through it. Class meetings provide a structured framework for giving students the opportunity and skills to do so.

A story from Monica's classroom illustrates the idea. As she was walking her kids out to the bus lines at the end of the day, one of her students, Jack, pulled on her hand and quietly said that he needed to tell her something. When she leaned down, this six-year-old boy whispered into her ear, "I'm afraid to get on my bus. That boy over there hits me in the head every day when he walks by me." After taking the rest of her students to their buses, Monica walked over to Chris, the fourth grader whom Jack had pointed out to her. She put her arm around his shoulder and said that one of her students wanted to talk to him.

For many of us, the temptation to "fix" Jack's problem for him (probably making it worse for him in the process) would have led us to confront Chris with the problem and threaten him with consequences. Instead, she walked Chris over to where Jack stood by the fence, trembling. She asked Jack to explain the problem to Chris. In a very small voice, Jack said, "I don't like it when you hit me in the head every day, when you walk past my seat when you get in trouble with the bus driver." Chris gave Jack and Monica an insolent look and shrugged. Monica asked him if it were true, that he hit Jack every day on the bus. Again, a sneer and a nonchalant shrug. Knowing that there wasn't time at the end of the day to work through the problem (and fighting the tempting but short-sighted impulse to march this bully straight to the office), Monica told Chris that she wanted him to come to her classroom the next day during their class meeting so they could work on the problem together. She said that if she heard from Jack that there was any hitting that night or the next morning on the bus, she wouldn't have any choice but to let the principal and his parents handle the problem, rather than giving him a chance to help take care of the situation himself. She walked the boys to their bus and asked the driver to keep a special eye out for Jack. She called Jack's parents that night to let them know what he was going through and to describe how she intended to help him the next day.

The next morning, Monica told Chris's teacher what had happened and asked her to send the boy to her classroom at 10:00 AM so he could join their class meeting. When he arrived, he sat behind the circle of kindergartners and first graders. Monica asked her students to make room for him, and after giving her a disbelieving look, Chris joined the circle, towering over the tiny people sitting around him. Her students were already in the process of naming the troubles they were having that week. When it was Jack's turn, he turned to Chris and said in a quavering voice, "I don't like it when you hit me on the bus. Why do you hit me?" Twenty-one children turned their wide-eyed faces to Chris, solemnly awaiting his reply. He sat, looking uncomfortable, saying nothing.

After giving him a moment, Monica asked Chris again if it were true. She reminded her students that they couldn't assume that he had done it without giving him a chance to respond to Jack. After Chris acknowledged in a surly tone that yeah, it was true, Jack asked him again why he did it. (One of the skills that Monica teaches her students to practice through class meetings is to find out for themselves why a problematic behavior is happening—to try to understand the other person's actions.) Silence. One of the kids started to suggest a possible reason for Chris's behavior, but Monica said that they needed to respect Chris and give him the time that he needed to think. Ten, twenty, and thirty seconds ticked slowly past.

Finally, responding to the weight of that focused silence, Chris grudgingly mumbled that sometimes he just felt angry and then he would hit people. Monica asked if he could think of anything else he could do besides hit when he became angry, but Chris just shrugged his shoulders. She asked her students if they had any thoughts, and in the next few minutes, nearly every student contributed an idea. One said, "You could just not be mad." Monica responded by defending Chris's right to be angry, drawing a quick, surprised look from him. Other students suggested things like "You could wait until you get home and then go for a run!" "You could go into your room and holler really loud into your pillow," and "You could talk to somebody about it." Through it all, Chris sat listening, looking uncomfortable but not overly invested in the process. When Monica asked him if he'd heard any suggestions that he thought he could use, he allowed after several seconds of more focused silence that he could probably talk to someone when he was angry. He then apologized to Jack. No one had asked him to do that. Monica asked her students to explain what they knew about what it means to say you're sorry, and they told Chris that if you're really sorry, you don't do it again.

Finally, Jack's turn was over and the group moved on to the next part of the meeting, when each person in the circle gave a compliment to someone in the class. When it came to Chris, he automatically turned to the child sitting next to him, assuming that his part in the meeting was over and that he wouldn't be expected to participate. Monica stopped and said, "I know you're new in our group today and you don't really know anyone, but can you think of any compliment for anyone here?" Realizing that the group would let him think for as long as it would take him to come up with something, Chris finally said to the children sitting around him, "I appreciate all of your ideas about how to help me."

After the meeting, Monica took Chris aside and asked him to come back to her classroom during the lunch recess. She explained that she just wanted him to spend some time with Jack, to get to know him a little. She said that she didn't believe that they needed to be friends, but that she didn't think it was okay for Chris to be picking on Jack and not even know him. She didn't tell Chris's teacher about this request, but he showed up right on time after lunch and spent the next 20 minutes putting puzzles together with Jack. Monica thanked him when he left, and she thought that was that. She planned to follow up later with Jack and his parents. To her surprise, Chris showed up at her door again later that day, asking if he could come in and play in her room during the afternoon recess.

Monica didn't fix Jack's problem. She taught him to confront it, to say what Chris was doing that he didn't like, even though it scared him to do it. She didn't leave him on his own with it at any point, though. She supported him and provided him with a safe, structured process to help him deal with a very real and scary problem. She didn't fix Chris's problem either, but she helped him with it. She didn't respond to his violence with threats of her own. She made him feel wanted, if uncomfortably so at first, in her classroom and in the process of finding a solution.

Class meetings provide teachers with opportunities to teach students problem-solving strategies for real-world applications. They can help students learn how to deal with their feelings, take responsibility for them, solve their own problems when they can, and ask for help when they need it. The simple act of letting students practice saying things like "Please stop doing that," "Why did you . . . ," and "I don't like it when you . . ." is an empowering use of class meeting time.

Kaia's weekly class meetings with fifth graders followed a procedure that her students helped to define. During the first meeting at the beginning of the year, she asked students to think about the rules they thought everyone should have to follow during these problem-solving and discussion sessions. The group came up with a set of rules (intentionally limited to three to force priorities and help them to be memorable) that were specific to class meetings: (1) only one person can talk at a time, and everybody else has to really listen, (2) people can talk only if they are explaining the problem or giving an idea (it can't be a time for complaining), and (3) what's said in the classroom stays there (except it's okay to share class meeting issues with parents at home).

Kaia introduced to her students the idea of an issue box, which was later labeled with their three class meeting rules. During the week, she kept a supply of blank issue forms handy, on which students with problems would provide a description of the problem and an explanation of what they had already done to try to solve it. (Class meeting time was never spent on a problem that hadn't already been worked on in some way.) Students decided that names on the issue slips should be optional, thinking that more kids would use the process for solving problems if they could do it anonymously.

Class meeting time was every Friday afternoon, 30 minutes before the afternoon recess. Kaia would initiate the meeting by asking students to review the three rules. Then she would read the first issue from the box. These she previewed during lunchtime to get a sense of that week's issues and to group them if similarities were obvious. The class used a rain stick to ensure that only one person could speak at a time; students would pass the stick to one another to determine speaking turns. Students' genuine engagement in the process was evident in the fact that problems were consistently solved throughout the year. Further, issue authors would almost always own their problem at some point during the class conversation about it. Finally, students would occasionally vote to give up their Friday afternoon recess so that they could continue working their way toward solutions for particularly compelling problems.

The power of class meetings for Kaia is illustrated in the story of Marcus, an aggressive boy who joined the class toward the end of the school year. Suddenly the issue box was filled to overflowing with Marcus problems. His behavior during class meetings was defensive and angry, and he seemed not to know how to react to classmates who, calmly and matter-of-factly, kept calling him on the things he was doing (like spitting at them during recess, swearing at them, and destroying their artwork and other papers). After his third week in the class, during a meeting that was again focused on problems with Marcus, Sarah finally said to him, "Marcus, you can keep on giving me that mean look, but you can't intimidate me. You don't scare me. I just want you to stop spitting at me." Marcus left the group in tears and went to his desk; two boys followed him and laid their arms across his shoulders as he cried. (By that point in the year, students were used to the idea that anger and tearfulness during class meetings might happen, that when conflicts were genuinely addressed, emotions might flare.) There were still incidents with Marcus during the last month of school, but he learned how to participate in class meetings and stopped being so constantly mean and aggressive.

One of the best benefits to class meetings from a teacher's perspective is that it removes her from the role of being the sole enforcer of class norms. When an issue being discussed is about one person having wronged another or if someone was caught breaking a school rule or classroom norm, the conversation can include what the consequences should be. Conversation about consequences should not take a long time; facilitation of this part of the discussion must be vigilant to keep it productively focused and to prevent it from becoming divisive.

What is striking about this aspect of class meetings is that older kids naturally understand the importance of logical consequences, and younger ones are easily coached to it. If some students suggest (as they did in Kaia's class) that a girl who wrote swear words with a permanent marker on the bathroom wall should have to write an apology to the principal, run laps, or write "I will not write on the bathroom wall" 100 times, someone else is bound to say, "That doesn't make any sense. If anyone should get an apology, it's the custodian and the other people who have to use the bathroom. And it would be better to make her clean it up herself than run around the playground or write a bunch of sentences."

In this particular instance, students thought that the girl shouldn't be made to tell her parents what she had done since she had confessed to the group that it was she who had done it. This was a defensible decision, from a child-centered perspective. Empowering students requires our faith in their abilities to learn on their own when it's appropriate—that is, when others' safety and well-being aren't jeopardized. Kids should be allowed to take responsibility for their actions without threat of additional consequences at home. This doesn't mean that we advocate keeping secrets from parents. To the contrary, sharing stories with parents that show how their child is learning to take responsibility for mistakes and bad decisions is a wonderful way to facilitate community development with them. (Chapter 6 discusses that topic in more depth.) What is just as striking is the fact that children who have a chance to participate in determining their own consequences are more likely to see them as fair and to accept them. The built-in barometer for fairness with which most kids seem thoroughly obsessed is honored well through the class meeting process.

Potential pitfalls with class meetings exist if clear guidelines are not established and if a teacher is not yet able to expect and facilitate respectful conversations consistently. Discussions about a particular problem can devolve into a complaining session if the teacher, as the meeting facilitator, is not firm about ensuring that comments are productively oriented (aimed at clarifying or solving the problem). There is also the risk that some students will subtly mock or ostracize the child who lacks popularity or social skills, if the teacher is unwilling or unable to call kids on such behavior. One way to do this is to ask, sincerely, "When you roll your eyes like that (or whatever it is that the student is doing), what would you actually be saying if you had to put that gesture into words?" Or, "Who are you sending that message to, and why?" It doesn't take many times of waiting long enough for an answer from one or two of these students before all of the kids have learned to avoid putting themselves in such an uncomfortable position. This doesn't guarantee students' positive regard for each other, of course, but by directly addressing and eliminating overtly disrespectful behaviors, the chances are better for a culture of kindness to take root.

Sometimes teachers may feel that they are protecting unpopular or friendless children by pretending not to see other students' ostracizing or excluding behaviors, but the unpopular or friendless student's only chance of figuring out how to belong is if she can get some help in dealing with what some of her peers are putting her through. She knows perfectly well what other kids are saying and doing to her, because when adults aren't around, those behaviors are far more blatant. Calling attention in a firm and fair way to mean-spirited facial expressions, gestures, and remarks at least lets students know that you see what is happening and that you are interested in helping all of them to belong and be their best selves. It also gives you a chance to model positive ways of confronting exclusionary and bullying behaviors, providing another opportunity to share responsibility with students for upholding community norms.

A final caution has to do with the student who thrives on negative attention, who can't seem to help but set himself up for his classmates' anger and frustration. Working privately with this student to help him find more productive ways to interact with his peers and, if necessary, to limit the number of issues he is permitted to submit in a week may help. If unchecked, class meetings can provide a student who seeks this kind of attention with a sanctioned stage for his drama. Allowing this child's issues to dominate the process will not help him to win friends, and it will discourage other students from investing themselves in the process. In every case, students who seem chronically unable to help others or be helped through class meetings or through your private work with them should be discussed with parents and other appropriate resources available at your school (e.g., the counselor, administrators, or the student assistance team). Be aware that a student's and family's right to confidentiality prohibits you from discussing the child by name or in other identifiable ways with colleagues or other miscellaneous persons who have no legal responsibility for the child.

While this approach to developing community is written from an elementary school perspective, it can be modified to be feasible and useful in middle and high school contexts as well. In view of the time constraints that teachers of adolescents typically face, McEwan (2000) suggested that weekly class meetings in the upper grades be limited to 15 minutes or held biweekly. Another option she described is to "form a representative group of students responsible for gathering topics of concern and interest to their peers. Teachers can meet with the representatives and use the meeting to set an agenda for a weekly or biweekly class meeting" (p. 67).

While 50-minute periods and responsibility for 100–125 students or more clearly make the challenge of community development a more difficult prospect than in the elementary classroom, the need is no less. Even in middle and high school classes, where time is all the more precious for its scarcity, a sense of community must be purposefully nurtured. Adolescents' deep and genuine engagement in their education is more possible in an environment of mutual respect and empowerment. Spending time on approaches that facilitate such an environment, we believe, effectively saves time in the long run. Think of the countless hours of seat time that many unengaged, uninspired secondary students log in the externally imposed interests of "covering" required, lockstep curricula. It is hard to imagine these kids being overly appreciative of all of the time that is "saved" when their needs and interests are sacrificed to curricular demands.

The idea that students must be fitted to schools dictates the frenzied pace of instruction in many elementary, middle school, and high school classrooms. This kind of thinking (from some of the most influential educational, political, and corporate leaders in America) encourages teachers to believe that there is simply no time for something as open-ended or "touchy-feely" as class meetings. In a society that is genuinely devoted to democratic ideals, this position is indefensible. A government of the people, by the people, and for the people presumes the existence of citizens who are able to communicate across their differences to make important decisions and solve difficult problems together. To make time for class meetings, whether in elementary, middle school, or high school settings, is to make time for the values inscribed in the Constitution. This is standards-based education—and this particular standard runs broad and deep. Citizenship is the province of every discipline.

Approach #6: Engage the class in activities that are specifically devoted to team building.

Particularly at the beginning of the year but also periodically throughout your months together, engage the class in team-building activities. Team builders provide fun, active opportunities for students to do things like learn each other's names (one way for students to feel a sense of belonging is for others to know their name; every person in the class should know everyone else's name at least by the end of the first week together); find out about each other's interests, ideas, and experiences (including yours); and support each other in accomplishing specific tasks. The goal is to give members of the community genuine opportunities to get to know and understand each other. Start building a repertoire of ice breakers and team builders; ideas and resources are plentiful online. Students who are given these opportunities, who are helped to find value in each other, are learning how to be respectful and open-minded people with a concern for the public good. They are also learning that getting to know each other is a lot of fun and a serious need in any community.

Helping children to get to know and value their classmates is a particularly important goal in view of the fact that so many of our students are actively engaged in unhealthy relationships with each other. It would be naïve to approach the challenge of building a classroom community without considering the extent to which bullying is a problem for our students. The National School Safety Center went so far as to say that it's "the most enduring and underrated problem in American schools" (Mulrine, 1999, p. 15). Research findings from the last decade solidly support that statement. Of American students, 10%–24% are bullied regularly at school, depending on whose research is cited (Garrity, Jens, Porter, Sager, & Short-Camilli, 1997; Leff, Left, Patterson, Kupersmidt, & Power, 1999; Mulrine, 1999; Weir, 2001), and 20% of schoolchildren report being frightened during much of their school day (Garrity et al., 1997). In one study, 43% of all students surveyed reported being afraid of using the bathroom at school because they were afraid of being harassed in this typically unsupervised haven for bullies (Mulrine as cited in Beale & Yilik-Downer, 2001). The problem is not for victims alone. Worldwide, 65% of boys identified as bullies by the second grade have a major criminal conviction by age 24 (Olweus as cited in Woodward, 1997), and 60% of bullies in grades six through nine have a criminal record by that age (Beale & Yilik-Downer, 2001).

Addressing the bully problem requires progressive thinking. By involving children in finding solutions, some schools have been successful in reducing the incidence of bullying (Garrity et al., 1997; Mulrine, 1999; Olweus et al. as cited in Hazler & Carney, 2000). Of the children in schools worldwide, 60%–85% are neither bullies nor victims (Mulrine; Garrity et al.), and by productively and safely involving this "caring majority" (Garrity et al.), the children who are involved in bullying can be supported in changing their behaviors. Being real with students; creating class norms together; facilitating regular class meetings that empower students to name, describe, clarify, and solve their own problems; and giving students genuine, ongoing opportunities to know and understand one another are strategies that can be effective in helping kids to reduce the incidence of put-downs, insults, threats, harassment, and bullying in their classroom and school environments. Through such strategies, progressive educators can do much to challenge the culture of fear and violence in which too many children are spending their lives. Maxine Greene (1995), education philosopher and founder of the Center for Social Imagination, the Arts, and Education affiliated with the Teachers College of Columbia University, put it this way:

> As teachers, we cannot predict the common world that may be in the making, nor can we finally justify one kind of community more than another. We can bring warmth into places where young persons come together, however; we can bring in the dialogues and laughter that threaten monologues and rigidity. (p. 43)

If you were to focus on just a few goals when it comes to facilitating community for your students, perhaps ensuring the presence of warmth, conversation, and laughter in your classroom would be the ones to choose. Students who feel safe, important, and comfortable enough not only to have something to say but to want to be heard are well positioned to learn.

SUMMARY

In this chapter, we have explored the importance of building a classroom community of learners. The following approaches can be implemented to facilitate this process:

- *Be real.* Speak with your students in the same tone that you use to speak with adults, demonstrating your respect for their intelligence.
- *Create class norms together.* Rather than imposing only your values for behavior on the class, involve your students in the process.

- *Don't stop when norms are named. Now teach your students how to take responsibility for them and to make them real.* The ultimate goal is to help children become responsible for their own behavior and learning. Norms become real when students own them through regular and ongoing opportunities to review, revise, and maintain them.
- *Cultivate a calm and patient manner while upholding class norms and other clearly stated expectations.* Consistency is the defining element of "the tipping point" when it comes to developing a genuine sense of community with the learners in your care.
- *Hold weekly class meetings.* No problem can be truly solved unless the people who own it get to work their own way through it. Class meetings provide a structured framework for giving students the opportunity and skills to do so.
- *Engage the class in activities that focus specifically on team building.* Students who are given genuine opportunities to get to know and understand each other, who are helped to find value in each other, are learning how to be respectful and open-minded people with a concern for the public good.

2

Classroom Organization

"When I figured out what was bugging me about that classroom, I started counting ceiling tiles," Arianna said one day, after she'd been asked by the Student Assistance Team to observe a student whose behaviors were becoming increasingly disruptive to her own and others' learning. It seemed an odd thing to say—but the more this veteran of middle school teaching talked, the more perfect sense it made.

"I was in there to observe Danica's behaviors, but I was immediately uncomfortable. Something was wrong, and I couldn't focus on Danica until I understood what was distracting me. I decided to expand my focus, and I started watching all of the kids—first individually and then as a whole group. Within seconds I spotted the elephant in the room that had been staring me in the face. Their movement in the classroom was so limited! The students took up too little space, somehow. So that's when I started counting ceiling tiles. I mentally mapped the classroom layout onto those ceiling tiles, and then I counted how many tiles were devoted to 'teacher stuff' and how many to 'kid stuff.' That's when I really understood what had been bothering me while I'd been trying to watch Danica; it was easier to see, somehow, in that two-dimensional grid on the ceiling.

"Two-thirds of the space in that room was occupied by teacher-centered things: her desk, her six filing cabinets, her bookshelves, her supply cabinet, her computer, her small group table. When I focused on watching the kids' movement patterns in the room, I saw that they never went into those spaces unless the teacher invited them there. Two-thirds of the room wasn't theirs."

Imagine that you are the parent of a very bright, very creative, 12-year-old girl who doesn't like school and who shows it in every way that she can. You understand what your daughter has explained to you: that her misbehavior and refusal to comply with teachers' expectations are intentionally designed to communicate her disapproval of a system that she perceives to be uncaring about her unique interests, her artistic abilities, and her questions (which tend to focus this year on the problem of social injustice in the world). You have also just moved and have learned that in your new school district, parents are invited to have input in determining their child's middle school team placement. As a person who is new to the school community, how will you figure out which team placement will be the best fit for your child this year?

Now imagine that you are a seventh-grade language arts teacher in this district. What do you see as the benefits and drawbacks of the district's policy of ensuring that all parents (not just those who are school and/or cultural insiders who know how to work the system) are to be included in making placement decisions? How can the process of getting parental input be conducted to keep it from devolving into a weird, competitive season of "teacher tryouts"? Finally, imagine that the leadership council at your middle school (made up of administrative, faculty, support staff, parent, and student representatives) has decided to propose the following idea at a faculty meeting: have open house nights for each grade level—without the teachers. Administrators will guide parents and incoming seventh graders through their prospective classrooms without offering any commentary about any of the seventh-grade teachers. Following their classroom tours, each parent will be invited to fill out a request form, noting their first and second choices for which middle school team they would like their child to join; they will also be asked to explain their reasons for believing those particular teaching teams would best match their child's personality and learning needs.

If this plan were implemented in your school, what would parents and students observing your classroom learn about *you* in the process?

Beliefs about what it means to teach and to learn are written into the very walls of our classrooms. Our philosophies of education are revealed and enacted in every aspect of the classroom environment. Anyone with an opportunity to study what we do with space, answering questions like the ones listed below, could infer much about our beliefs and values. Whether parents should have formal opportunities to get to know us in this way and to have a voice in predicting whether our various personal and pedagogical styles will serve their children's needs effectively is another question altogether—one that we believe would be a rich topic for discussion by educators and parents in every school. If nothing else, this question underscores the inappropriate division that commonly exists between "us" and "them," which in itself should catapult it onto the list of things that parents and educators should be discussing together.

FINDING YOU IN YOUR CLASSROOM

Your general philosophy of education is apparent to anyone with access to your classroom who can take the time to consider thoughtfully at least four of its aspects: the floor plan, the wall plan, the internal structures, and the emotional environment. What kind of a teacher would Danica and her parents see in you, if all they had to go on was a tour of your classroom and the following questions to guide them?

Floor Plan: How is the furniture arranged?
Who owns the floor space?

1. What is the seating arrangement like? What does it help students to see, to focus on, and to do? (If the seating arrangement is dictated by the need to fit 40 bodies into a space designed for 25, who owns that decision, and how can parents be productively engaged in sharing responsibility for it?)

2. How are adults' needs for space accommodated?

3. How does furniture placement impact students' opportunities for movement in the room?

4. What choices does it appear that students can make given how the floor plan is designed?

5. Does the furniture arrangement allow for individual, small-group, and large-group instruction?

6. How does the floor plan promote and/or inhibit community development in the classroom?

Wall Plan: What is on the walls?
Who owns the wall space?

1. Is students' work visible? If not, whose is?

2. What is on the walls in addition to students' work? What purposes do those things appear to serve? Food for thought: If it

appears that much of the wall space is consumed by district-mandated materials (e.g., posters from packaged curricula or lists of standards that all students are expected to achieve in unison), who owns that space? For whom or what are students working, if ownership of the learning environment isn't theirs?

3. If students' work is displayed: What kinds of things are students shown doing in this class? Do student-produced artifacts on the walls indicate assignments that are open-ended and/or closed-ended? Are they the result of invitations to originality and/or to conformity? Does it appear that students have opportunities to grapple with genuine, relevant questions and challenges?

4. If students' work is visible: Are only finished products posted, or is there evidence that students can also see what messy work-along-the-way drafts look like? Does any other evidence indicate whether mistakes and revisions are valued as part of the learning process? Are the efforts of all students honored?

5. How do the materials on the walls promote and/or inhibit community development in the classroom?

Internal Structures: What norms and routines are in place? Is it evident who owns them?

1. If class norms (i.e., rules and expectations) are posted: What do they communicate about the teacher's leadership style? Could a visitor infer from how they are written whether students had input in identifying, defining, or representing/communicating them?

2. What other evidence is available to suggest the academic, social, cultural, and behavioral values in this classroom?

3. Is it evident that routine procedures are in place for day-to-day activities in the classroom (e.g., checkout system for using the bathroom, sign-up system for choosing learning centers)? What evidence exists to suggest that students understand those procedures, or that they participated in defining them?

4. What routines appear to be in place for managing learning materials and supplies? Do all materials and supplies seem to have clear places to belong in the classroom? Do students have access to them? If so, will they be able to tell where/how to put them away?

5. How do the evident norms, routine procedures, and organizational system for managing learning materials and supplies promote and/or inhibit community development in the classroom?

Emotional Environment: What is the tone of the room?

1. What emotions or attitudes do the environmental conditions in this classroom evoke? How does the room *feel* on various continuums (e.g., welcoming or uninviting, joyful or cheerless, warm or cold, calm or tense, fun or oppressive, cooperative or competitive, learner-centered or teacher-centered)? What specific things in the room contribute to these inferences?

2. What evidence suggests how students are treated? Is an orientation toward intrinsic motivation and personal responsibility evident, or does there appear to be more of an emphasis on hierarchical control (i.e., punishments and rewards)? Does it appear that public attention is drawn to individual students' behaviors (e.g., names on the board, pulling yellow/red "tickets"), making reminders of behavioral successes and failures visible to others?

   More food for thought: The practice of making students' behavioral performances visible to classroom members as well as to visitors is widely accepted and commonly practiced, but other behavioral performances, like homework completion and test results, are legally prohibited from being publicized. Is the publication of any kind of behavioral performance legally defensible?

3. What evidence suggests the degree of inclusiveness that is practiced in this classroom? Does it appear that the diverse cultures, experiences, abilities, and interests of all students are genuinely appreciated and accessed in the day-to-day processes of teaching and learning?

The four categories named above (floor plan, wall plan, internal structures, and emotional environment) provide the framework we will use in defining strategies for organizing a learner-centered classroom. This conceptual approach will not offer such things as the sample floor plans often found in a number of helpful guides to classroom organization; rather, our thought is that general guidelines for organization that are appropriate for all grade levels can be framed by the goals identified in the four categories named above.

FROM THEORY TO PRACTICE: STRATEGIES FOR ORGANIZING A LEARNER-CENTERED CLASSROOM

Approach #1: Ensure that the floor plan encourages student interaction, community development, ease of movement, and a variety of options for teaching and learning.

> *Create a seating plan that reflects your understanding of students as social beings and that promotes conversation, cooperation, and peer coaching.*

Ideally, involve students in creating this aspect of the floor plan (which can change periodically over the course of the year, if you are ambitious about providing environmental stimulation). Martín, a fourth-grade teacher, assigns the job of redesigning the seating/ furniture configuration to a different student team each month. These teams do their planning outside of class time and must get his approval before they can implement their ideas. On the day that he signs off on the plan, the team spends their lunch period in the classroom. Martín eats with them, then works at his desk while the students rearrange furniture.

A related topic is that of seating assignments. When given complete freedom to choose their own seats, kids (like adults) generally segregate into groups based on things like friendship, gender, race, and perceptions of popularity. A learner-centered approach to this topic does not imply that students must have total freedom to choose their seats. The emphasis, as ever, is on being learner-centered, which means that always allowing students to stay within their comfort zones will be counterproductive to learning (in this case, social learning) and growth. At the same time, we recognize how fun and comfortable it is to sit with *our* friends during staff meetings and conferences, and we believe that fun and comfort are as essential to kids' experiences in school as they are to our own. Our thought, which may again reflect a more moderate than radical-progressive perspective, is that a fair approach recognizes both needs: for teachers to ensure that student groupings serve social and academic learning goals, and for students to have choices.

Martín, whose approach to seating configurations is designed to address both his and his students' needs, has a similarly balanced approach to seat assignments. He sets up the parameters (for example, there must be both girls and boys in each cluster of seats). Then he draws popsicle sticks with students' names on them, and kids choose their seats when their name is drawn. He promises the two students whose sticks were drawn last that they will have first and second pick the next time seat assignments are changed.

While our bias is obviously in favor of seating arrangements that put students in contact with each other (tables or clusters of desks, rather than rows), we also recognize the needs of some children to have their own space. This does not mean that we advocate segregating students with Attention Deficit Hyperactivity Disorder who have difficulty concentrating, for example, or that students in wheelchairs cannot be included in seating clusters. Perish the thought. It does mean that when the need for separate space is indicated by the student (either by choice or by failing to behave cooperatively and/or safely around others), we accommodate it by providing isolated areas that individuals can use on a temporary basis, as the need arises.

We are also alert, however, to times when children repeatedly choose to work alone because they want to avoid the challenges of cooperating with others and developing interpersonal skills, or because they feel superior to other students, or because they do not feel liked. When personal rather than academic needs are met by being separated from others, it is necessary to understand the problem and help the child to work through it. Having an isolated seating option is also necessary so that you can temporarily remove a student from the group whose behavior is disruptive or hurtful to others. It is important to make sure that this student understands that she has the power to rejoin the group when she is willing to fix whatever problem she has caused and can demonstrate that other children will be safe in her company.

Create a floor plan that allows for instructional grouping options.

In addition to planning seating arrangements and seat assignments that will facilitate students' individual and cooperative work as well as large-group instruction, make sure that you have at least one space in which you can conference with a small number of students (e.g., coaching a group of five kids who are ready to learn how to use quotation marks and to organize paragraphs in a dialog, or who are all struggling with understanding why and how to divide fractions, or who are reading the same novel in their reading group). Also, create a space or make a plan for rearranging furniture to accommodate class meetings. Ideally, this arrangement would allow everyone to sit in a circle, a semicircle, or in concentric semicircles so that faces are more easily visible to every person.

Analyze the floor plan while students are using it throughout the year to check for unforeseen or newly developing problems.

By thinking of the space in your room as an instructional resource, you can learn to see each area in terms of its usefulness throughout the day. If a certain area is firmly defined by one activity and then sits unused for the rest of the day, a spatial resource is being squandered. The challenge is to maximize the amount of space that can be utilized throughout the day by creating spaces that can be used for multiple purposes. This may require learning to think differently about the furniture in your room. A teacher's desk doesn't always have to be a teacher's desk, for example; it can be a writing center or a math center, with a designated drawer used for storing whatever supplies kids need to do their work there. Monica's approach is to use a chart cabinet as her "desk." It houses all kinds of classroom supplies, and its surface provides her with the workspace she needs during the day. At the same time, it is clear that some space must be designated for teacher use only (e.g., lockable cabinets for securing personal items and confidential student files).

Use the following questions to guide your analysis of the spatial resources represented in your floor plan: (1) Which areas of the room do students use routinely? Are any areas consistently unused or underutilized? Why? (2) Are there any congested areas in the room, where too many students are trying to move in too small of a space? (3) Are any students consistently distracted? What is causing the distraction? (4) Do students have easy access to the learning materials and supplies that they need? (5) Can you see all students from wherever you are in the room? Can all students see you easily during large-group instruction? Finally, what solutions can the students and/or you find in response to any problems you identify through your floor plan analysis?

Be extremely conscious about how much of the room is taken up with things that serve mainly adult needs.

You and any other adults in the room must have space for doing your work and storing personal things. As a matter of fact, one way that you can encourage educational assistants, student teachers, and parent volunteers to feel like valued members of the classroom community is to ensure that their needs for personal space are recognized and addressed. However, as the opening story to this chapter illustrates, it's possible for adults to claim too much of the classroom as theirs. These people tend to be more devoted to establishing an excellent teaching environment than to ensuring the excellence of the learning environment. In many classrooms, for example, one of the few computers in the room is located on the teacher's desk—off-limits to students and therefore typically unused during most of the school day. This is a provocative illustration of adults' needs being served at the expense of the other members in the learning community. By creating password-protected files and documents, teachers' privacy needs can be served without costing students access to a valuable resource. While adults' spatial needs absolutely must be honored, care must also be taken to ensure that they don't encroach on students' fair share of the room.

Approach #2: Ensure that the wall space is purposefully used to highlight students' accomplishments and originality; to provide students with tools and guidelines that will facilitate their success, independence, and cooperation; and to promote the social and academic values of the community.

> *Make sure that the things students are working on in your classroom are things you'd be thrilled to have students, parents, educators, and other community members see on the wall.*

You can highlight students' accomplishments and originality only if they have opportunities to tackle genuinely challenging projects creatively. Most of us have seen the sad rows of identical pumpkin cutouts adorning the wall outside of a primary classroom in October, distinguishable only by the level of fine-motor development evident in the cutting and coloring. When the most important choices about students' projects are made for them, one can only cheer for the kid who decided on a purple pumpkin. Training starts early for accepting the parameters and possibilities that others define for our lives.

While there is clear value in young children's being able to practice using scissors and learning their colors, there is an equally valid need to offer them open-ended academic and artistic opportunities to explore what they know and can do. A child who gets to see his work only in comparison to the identical assignments completed by the other 24 children in the class is learning the importance of perfection. He needs to see evidence that his unique ways of knowing and doing are valued, too. Giving students opportunities to tackle genuinely challenging projects creatively gives you the chance to publish results on your classroom and school walls for an audience that will enjoy them as individual, rather than collective, representations of learning.

> *Let students see constant evidence of your belief that mistakes and revisions are valuable and necessary for learning.*

Post samples of what the *entire* writing process looks like, maybe even with a piece of your own writing. You will be sending a powerful message by letting students see a sample of your handwritten brainstorming web (or quick-write or outline), your first draft (complete with a mess of crossed-out and rearranged phrases, sentences, and paragraphs with mechanical errors identified with basic editing marks), second draft (and possibly your third or fourth), and your final version, all "published" on the wall. We know that many children stop pursuing artistic development when they become conscious of the "right" way of representing ideas and objects. You can help the children in your care to resist the everyday tyranny of the right and narrow by posting a wider variety of things on the wall than exemplars of conformity and perfection. At the same time, by posting messy work-along-the-way drafts, you can help them to see when learning "right ways" is essential in serving important learner-centered goals (e.g., social power has much to do with the ability to use language correctly and well).

> *Use wall space to promote the values of community, inclusion, and cooperation as well as those of individuality, diversity, and independence.*

Walter Parker (1996) defined the challenge of democracy as the ongoing process of finding balance between the human conditions of mutuality and diversity. Students need help to become conscious of these competing and complementary values in a democratic society. They need opportunities to develop the skills to be both independent and cooperative, to be respectful of difference yet united in supporting everyone's right to belong. Wall space can be used to help students to become aware of the challenge of balancing the sometimes competing, sometimes complementary interests of the personal and the public good. Specific tools can be posted for helping students to develop knowledge and skills both individually and cooperatively. Word walls can help students to become independent writers, for example, while a posted rubric defining effective and ineffective group membership can help them to develop collaborative skills.

If your school or district mandates what is to be posted on the walls of your classroom, find ways to insert your students into the process.

While a radical progressive's response to administrative, political, or corporate ownership of classroom wall space would be to challenge it directly or subvert it indirectly, our concern in this instance is for the new teacher who doesn't yet believe he has the political or professional clout to engage in overt or covert acts of resistance. If your school or district requires that you post the standard that all students are to achieve simultaneously in a given week or month, go ahead and post it. But post student work more prominently—work that celebrates your students' efforts relative to that (or a related) standard. If you are required to tack up the poster of the week from the packaged reading program that your school or district has adopted, go ahead. But feature your reading center more prominently—and provide anything that you can get your hands on to put in that center and in the rest of your classroom to show students that it's the *doing* of reading that matters (e.g., a tape recorder with the direction that each student is to record herself reading for a certain number of minutes each week on her personal cassette; or prerecorded readings of that day's science, social studies, or short story text along with a listening center that five or six kids can plug into at the same time). In our view, it's not worth the risk of having a spectacularly short career in education to do battle over these kinds of mandates. Find, read, and take to heart Herbert Kohl's essay (1994) on "creative maladjustment" instead.

Approach #3: Ensure that behavioral expectations, routine procedures, and an organizational system for managing learning materials and supplies are clearly established and communicated (with meaningful opportunities for students' participation).

Ask students to create things that represent and communicate class norms (e.g., posters, mobiles, bulletin boards, and photographs of skits and other performances) and post these in the room.

Create and maintain class norms with students (see Chapter 1) and give them responsibility for representing these shared goals (i.e., their view of the common good) in the classroom. Performances like skits and songs illustrating the significance of specific norms can be captured in photographs that become part of the class history that is posted on the walls.

> *Involve students whenever possible in establishing procedures for routine parts of the day and in creating any accompanying documents or directions that are necessary for each one.*

A learner-centered classroom is not a chaotic one in which students are free to "express themselves" whenever and however they wish. Instead, children's needs for predictability are consciously honored, and these needs are addressed with whatever level of help each child is capable of offering. Older students might be divided into teams, each of which is assigned the job of planning a different procedure that has been identified as a need by you and/or by them. Younger students' involvement might be more appropriately addressed in whole-class discussions in class meetings or through creating illustrations of procedures that you have designed. As in all things, students must have opportunities to practice new procedures before being expected to follow them independently. The common argument against involving students in these kinds of decisions, that there is insufficient time to address standards and allow children to collaborate in defining their environment, is easily countered if you can point with confidence to the language arts, social studies, and art standards you will be addressing through this kind of learning activity.

> *Put learning materials and supplies where students can get to them and label those storage spaces clearly (with pictures, too, when necessary) so that students can be responsible for returning supplies to where they belong.*

You might be an incredibly organized person, but if you are the only one taking responsibility for retrieving and returning supplies, your students are missing out on an opportunity to learn how to be independent, responsible stewards of their learning and of their environment. If you find yourself restoring the room to order at the end of every day, it is possible that students have not been given enough guidance and/or responsibility for taking care of their classroom. This situation offers a perfect opportunity for you to name and define the problem in a class meeting and to engage students in solving it (e.g., devise a procedure or develop a rubric to guide students' evaluations of personal and group performance in that area).

Approach #4: Ensure (as best you can) that the physical elements of the room are consistent in promoting a respectful, welcoming, joyful, warm, calm, fun, cooperative, and learner-centered approach to teaching and learning.

Be conscious of environmental elements that put you and your students at ease, and try to build a version of those elements into your classroom.

A lamp, an area rug, classical music during quiet times, an electric waterfall, an overstuffed chair, a wall for everyone's family photographs, a class pet, plants—use anything (not restricted by school/district policy) that will help you to communicate the idea that this room is a safe, welcoming, and fun place to be.

Analyze your room for message consistency.

The following questions can guide your analysis: (1) Does anything in the room communicate the idea that only some students belong there? (A teacher we know used to have a sign posted beside the door that was entitled "Sped Kids," and it listed their pullout times and services. Awareness of legality, not human decency, prompted her to remove the sign.) (2) Does anything represent any form of public reporting of behavioral or academic performance? (3) Does anything in the classroom promote a competitive rather than cooperative atmosphere? Are students encouraged to feel good or bad about themselves in comparison to how other students are doing? (4) Is there evidence that students had a voice and a hand in creating the environment? (5) Does anything in the room detract from its feeling like a respectful, welcoming, joyful, warm, calm, fun, and learner-centered place?

When you are learner-centered, classroom organization is about creating spaces that make everyone feel welcome, valued, and safe enough to take the risks that are necessary for all group members to be able to do their best work. From this perspective on organization, a teacher is an interior designer who is responsible for addressing the emotional, social, cognitive, and physical needs of every person in the room. Becoming an effective designer of a learning environment—figuring out how to organize your classroom around the needs of your students—will take time and the purposeful cultivation of reflective and analytical thought. Only by carefully watching what your students do, by attending to how they move in the classroom and make use of the spaces available to them throughout the year, will you be able to tell if the organizational structure you've designed is consistently serving them well.

SUMMARY

The organization of your classroom is a reflection of your general philosophy of education. The following strategies for organizing a learner-centered classroom environment were discussed in this chapter:

- Develop a floor plan that encourages student interaction, community growth, ease of movement, and a variety of options for teaching and learning.
- Purposefully use wall space to highlight students' accomplishments and originality; to provide students with tools and guidelines that will facilitate their success, independence, and cooperation; and to promote the social and academic values of the community.
- Establish and clearly communicate behavioral expectations, routine procedures, and an organizational system for managing learning materials and supplies. Involve students whenever possible in establishing procedures for routine parts of the day.
- Ensure (as best you can) that the physical elements of the room are consistent in promoting a respectful, welcoming, joyful, warm, calm, fun, cooperative, and learner-centered approach to teaching and learning.

3

Observing and Assessing What Students Know and Can Do

Jamie was asked if she thought the word progressive was a meaningful word to use in describing herself as a teacher. Her reply was interesting—and very much aligned with John Dewey's ideas about what it means to be an educator. "I don't actually define myself as a teacher!" she said. "I never have. I see myself as a scientist who teaches.

"I think some of it's my training," she explained. "I have a bachelor's and a master's in science, and I've done research in the sciences. I've trained to be a laboratory researcher. So I think I bring to education those skills of observation and of analyzing and synthesizing information to make sense of it. And I do the same thing in education. I observe students. I observe how they learn, and I use that to solve problems.

"I think that's why I'm drawn to working with kids with behavioral issues, because to me, that's incredibly challenging. I love working with kids with behavioral issues, because there's that whole challenge of developing hypotheses about what's causing the behavior. I look at it as an experiment. If I run this experiment and try this intervention, what's likely to happen? And then I'm collecting the data and revisiting the hypothesis. So that's how I approach it.

"And that's how I try to present it to the education students I teach. I don't know where they have gotten this idea, but they are so convinced that as the teacher, they have to know everything, so they're afraid to run those experiments. In their minds—because they are the teacher—they have to identify, the first time, the cause for the behavior. They have to identify, the first time, the appropriate intervention for the behavior. And what

I try to tell them is, every time you run that experiment, you now have more information to develop a better experiment. And then you'll be more likely to get the outcome that you want if you do this process of hypothesizing, conducting the experiment, analyzing the results, and then revisiting the hypothesis to determine whether or not it was accurate. If so, great. If not, then you develop a new hypothesis based on this new set of data that you now have."

Whether we are guiding students' behavior or helping them develop content knowledge and skills, Jamie's approach to teaching suggests the key to where it all begins. Her emphasis is on learning to see each child well enough to understand what he needs and then to generate ideas that can be tested for their usefulness to that child. This emphasis on experimentation is not one of cold detachment but of serving students intelligently and effectively. Whether you see yourself as a teacher or as a scientist who teaches, your success with the children in your care will depend to a large degree on your own "scientific" skills: those that will help you to see your students well enough to understand their individual needs.

This chapter is based on three assumptions: (1) you can't teach someone you don't know, (2) you will assess what you value, (3) you will never finish the project of learning how to be a skilled observer and assessor of your students' knowledge and abilities. Each of these assumptions will be explored in the following pages.

UNDERSTANDING TERMINOLOGY

Observation and *assessment* are related terms: observation is actually a form of assessment. When you *observe* a student and when you *assess* her performance in a variety of realms within the areas of academic and social development, you are essentially doing the same thing: you are gathering information, either formally or informally, to help her develop the new knowledge and skills that she has demonstrated her readiness to learn.

While a teacher who is not a careful observer/assessor of his students can often be described as primarily content oriented, one who does believe in and act upon the instructional importance of assessment can be described as primarily student centered. The former uses assessment opportunities primarily to evaluate the degree to which students have mastered content knowledge and skills; the latter believes that content evaluation, while obviously essential, is a less important assessment goal than knowing his students. This teacher's primary assessment goal is to know his students well enough to understand what they need from him to achieve ever more sophisticated levels of understanding and skill. The point here is not that content knowledge is unimportant to a learner-centered teacher; rather, it is through this teacher's student-centered orientation that content is most effectively served. In short, the primarily content-oriented teacher sees the value of assessment in terms of informing evaluation; the primarily child-centered teacher values this purpose highly also, but he sees it as secondary to the more essential purposes of informing his instruction and facilitating students' ownership of their learning.

One of the implied messages in the preceding paragraph is that assessing and evaluating students are two entirely different processes. To reiterate this important distinction: assessment entails the collection of data, whether through the use of formal instruments (e.g., diagnostic reading tests, performance rubrics, paper-and-pencil tests, behavior scales) or through the typically less formal processes of observing students' behaviors and recording anecdotal notes. The primary purpose of assessment for the child-centered teacher, then, is *formative* (to shape learning and teaching processes) rather than *summative* (to judge performance). The goal of assessment is to find out what the student does and does not yet understand, to discover what she can and cannot yet do, to help the child to learn. In this way, assessment serves the essential function of informing instruction.

Another important purpose of assessment for the progressive educator is to facilitate the student's ownership of her own education by involving her in assessing and reflecting upon her own performance. Student assessment serves a third purpose of allowing teachers and students to communicate specific, detailed information to parents about the child's academic and social development. Finally, assessment data are required for the essential purpose of evaluating students' content knowledge and skills.

Assessment information also serves the purpose of informing district, state, and federal evaluations of students, teachers, and schools, but our concern is with assessment and evaluation practices that impact the actual processes of teaching and learning and, thus, are relevant at the level of classroom experience.

Evaluation follows assessment. Evaluation involves the making of judgments relative to a pre-established set of criteria, using the information obtained through various formal and informal assessments. Assigning letter grades, establishing a child's current level of performance as a writer according to a rubric of developmental stages, determining whether or not a student qualifies for special services, and deciding to place a student in honors or remedial English (the effects of tracking students by ability level will be discussed briefly in Chapter 7) are examples of evaluative decisions that teachers make. While we see evaluation as a fourth essential purpose for assessing students' knowledge and skills, it tends to be the one that gets the most attention in schools, in homes, and in the press. Evaluations represent official judgments of students' abilities. What distinguishes the progressive educator from traditionalists in this area is his determination to include students in the process of arriving at these judgments—of ensuring that his students are subjects in the process rather than objects of it. The topics of evaluating and reporting student growth are developed further in Chapter 5. The remainder of this chapter will be devoted to the why, when, and how of assessing what students know and can do.

ASSUMPTION #1: YOU CAN'T TEACH SOMEONE YOU DON'T KNOW

While it is entirely possible to train strangers in large groups or small, teaching requires trusting relationships and detailed knowledge of what students already know and can do. Unless a teacher knows her students as individual learners, even a well-intentioned, would-be progressive educator can aim only generic lessons in her students' general direction and hope for the best. Through knowing our students, appropriate instructional goals are revealed. Only through knowing them does the possibility of individualized, differentiated instruction become conceivable.

An illustration of this idea lies in our observation that the older a student is, sadly, the less likely his teachers are to know detailed information about his abilities as a reader. Traditionally oriented secondary teachers commonly assess students' knowledge in the content areas they teach, but they typically have no formal knowledge of their students' reading levels. They aren't generally encouraged to assess or teach reading skills; unfortunately, it's common knowledge that secondary teachers are typically responsible for teaching content, not reading. The problem is that a content orientation effectively normalizes the expectation that all children develop at the same pace. Therefore when middle and high school children "fail," the traditional, content-oriented teacher feels justified in believing that it is her students, their parents, and their previous teachers who are deficient. A child-centered secondary teacher, by contrast, is not interested in justifying failure but in understanding how previous failures will inform his relationship and his instructional approach with that student. He would agree with Herbert Kohl (1994), who wrote,

> "Failure" has a prominent place in the vocabulary of educational experts, although I don't believe it is a useful educational category. It does not help one teach, and it inhibits and suppresses learning. For example, children who cannot read at levels they are expected to simply cannot do certain things. Calling them failures tags an insult onto a statement of fact. We stigmatize their current inability by articulating it into a norming system when we should be going about inventing new ways to help students instead. (p. 75)

Through exploring the extent of what his students know and can do, the learner-centered teacher is equipped to teach individuals.

ASSUMPTION #2: YOU WILL ASSESS WHAT YOU VALUE

Being able to articulate clear social and academic goals for the children in your care is essential to establishing and implementing an effective assessment plan. Preservice and beginning teachers are often coached to be "kid watchers," but they may not be helped to understand what they should actually be watching *for*. By naming, prioritizing, and documenting progress toward the varying social and academic goals that you have for each of your students, you will be creating an assessment map, so to speak. On the other hand, if you spend the year with your students without articulating specific learning goals, you will have no established criteria for directing your assessment efforts. Observation and other strategies for gathering information about your students' knowledge and skills then become generalized, vague, and aimless exercises rather than critical components of your assessment plan. Clearly stated social goals (e.g., treating others with respect, being able to cooperate and collaborate in a group) and academic goals (e.g., writing a focused and well-organized paragraph, explaining and applying the correct order of mathematical operations) provide you with direction and focus, a specific map to follow when observing and otherwise assessing individual students.

Another point to make here is that kids are natural detectors of contradictions and inconsistencies. If you say that you value respectful, thoughtful cooperation and collaboration but you assess and evaluate students' individual work only, it won't take them long at all to figure out what you actually believe is important. We assess what we value. We also give value to what we assess, meaning that students are helped to internalize the importance of learning goals when they see us spending time on assessing progress toward those goals, particularly when we engage them in the process. Any student who has labored over an assignment only to have it returned with the sole comment of "Great job! A+" at the top has probably had the experience of wondering whether her teacher even bothered to read her work. That same student is likely to attach more value to the assignment and the learning goals it addresses if she sees that her teacher has taken time to respond thoughtfully—to offer comments that address particular strengths of the work as well as appropriately challenge or push the student toward new learning. We assess what we value, and we give value to what we assess.

This is not to say that a student's inability to honor all class norms, for example, should be reflected in his grade—even though you obviously value adherence to those norms. If you must give letter grades, they should reflect students' progress toward academic goals. The relevant point here is that giving value to what we assess can happen in ways that do not involve grades. By spending time on those community norms, involving students in their creation and maintenance, you will be giving value to them. If you encourage students to believe that cooperation and collaboration are important values, they will know only that you mean it if you spend time accordingly—gathering information with them about their cooperative and collaborative abilities and then teaching them how to use that data, reflecting on it to further develop those skills. You will know that you have been successful in facilitating the development of a genuine community of learners when you and your students are more interested in growing than in grading.

ASSUMPTION #3: YOU WILL NEVER FINISH LEARNING HOW TO ASSESS STUDENTS' KNOWLEDGE

All new students who come to you will obviously bring their own sets of experiences, understandings, and skills with them. All will be unique in terms of how willing and able they are to let you see these things, to show you the evidence of who they are and of what they know and can do. Because of this, your skills as an assessor of students' knowledge and skills will never be finalized, only honed over the years with intentional practice.

The more teachers are encouraged to standardize their expectations and their teaching practices, and the more they are taught to believe that their responsibility is to focus on content rather than individual children, the more difficulty they will have honing their skills as observers and assessors of students' academic performances. When teachers' eyes are overly focused on the curriculum, they cannot fully see their students. The learner-centered educator seeks first to know his students and then to apply curricular goals—which he knows like the back of his hand—accordingly. If observation and other forms of assessment can be thought of as one aspect of the science of teaching, then the application of appropriate curricular goals for each member in a community of learners is its counterpart in the art of teaching.

Finding the balance between science and art is a complicated challenge for every teacher. New teachers must be encouraged to be patient with themselves in this, because finding that balance will take a while. They also need to be encouraged to be forgiving of themselves, because mistakes will be necessary in finding the way. This is hard for a lot of us. Our best advice is to let your kids in on some of your mistakes—parents, too, when necessary. By naming aloud your inevitable mistakes, you will gain power over them by externalizing them; you will also be modeling the kind of learning that you want your students to feel safe enough to do. When mistakes are not named and owned, they have a tendency to gain more and more power with every mental replay. The best way to put those torturous internal movies into perspective is to get them outside of you. Name them, apologize if you need to, and move on with the new knowledge you've gained.

FROM THEORY TO PRACTICE: STRATEGIES FOR ASSESSING WHAT STUDENTS KNOW AND CAN DO

Approach #1: Enjoy the challenge of becoming a skilled observer and assessor of your students' knowledge and abilities.

Assessment is like an encrypted conversation between students and their teacher. You cannot know what your part in the conversation should be until you know what your students are telling you—through their mistakes and successes, through their actions and their words, through their frustrations and celebrations. Seen in this way, instruction is the conversational response to assessment. Let yourself enjoy the puzzle of figuring out what your lines should be! Be a sleuth in your teaching, not an automaton programmed only to respond to the frenzied demands of the curriculum and the state's testing regimen. One of the things that makes a teacher great is his ability to figure out what underlies his students' behaviors and beliefs. Alfie Kohn (1999) explained:

> [I]f a child announces that four plus five equals ten, the teacher doesn't have to say "Wrong!" or "Ooh, you're close; try again" (a nicer way of saying "Wrong!"). Sarcastic claims by traditionalists notwithstanding, that doesn't mean the teacher is obliged to say, "OK, sure, honey, if that's a valid answer for you, we'll all say it's ten." Not at all. The teacher might simply ask, "How'd you get ten?" Alternatively, he could ask, "Did anyone else get a different answer? Let's talk about it." What's more, both of these responses are just as appropriate when a child announces that four plus five equals nine. It may be even more important to help students reflect on—and therefore allow the teacher to understand—how they got the *right* answer. (p. 138)

Progressive, child-centered teachers enjoy the challenge of discovering their students and exploring the mysteries that they are.

Approach #2: Let students inside the assessment process.

The simple power of this approach is illustrated in the following story. Several years ago, Kaia was working as an elementary school principal in Kodiak, Alaska. One of her responsibilities was to coordinate the writing assessment project for K–8 students throughout the school district. On one particular morning in May, she was working with a group of primary-level teachers; the group was in the process of refining the "Developmental Stages of Primary Writing" rubric they had drafted, and they were using it to evaluate papers from all of the K–2 students in the district. Before the day's work had begun, Kaia noticed two teachers sitting in the back of the room: one was talking and looking upset, and the other was listening intently.

Finally, the listener said, "Margaret, you just have to tell everyone this story!" So encouraged, Margaret shared what was troubling her. This was the story she told.

I was talking to my students yesterday afternoon, explaining to them why I was going to be out of the classroom for the next two days. I said, "Remember back in the fall when I was gone for two days? When a bunch of other teachers and I got together to look at your writing papers that you did? Well, we're going to do that again tomorrow and Friday. We'll be assessing the papers that you wrote a few days ago." As soon as I said that, Peter, one of my particularly streetwise second graders, shot his hand up in the air.

"You're going to correct all our mistakes, huh?" he said knowingly.

"Oh, no," I said. "We're not going to mark on them at all. We just want to look at them to see where you all are in your work at becoming good writers."

"Well, how can you tell that if you don't mark up all our mistakes?" he asked.

"We'll be using this rubric," I explained. I had a copy of it right there on my desk, along with the class reports that we'd gotten back from the fall assessment. I held the rubric up and showed them how it worked. I explained that we'd used it to look at each student's progress in two areas, Story Sense and Conventions, and I explained what those two traits were about. I showed them how each of those traits was defined by eight separate stages of development. I said that the rubric was an important tool for teachers to have since we knew that students would be in different places on it; we knew that they grew as writers at different times, just as they had all learned to walk and talk at different times when they were little.

Peter eyed that fall report in my hand and asked, "Where am I on that?"

My whole class was gathered around me, and I knew I shouldn't talk about a student's progress in front of other kids. But he had asked me, and I could see how curious all of my students were about the whole conversation. I couldn't not answer his question! So I showed them how all of them were listed on my fall report, and I looked up Peter's name. I said, "Back in the fall, Peter, we thought you were at Stage 5 in your development of Story Sense and at Stage 4 in Conventions." Then I read what the rubric says about Stage 5 in Story Sense ("Writes sentences that generally stay on a single topic; may display in writing a sense of beginning and ending; communicates meaning to the reader.") and Stage 4 in Conventions ("Attempts transitional spelling using some consonants; may use some vowels; may write left to right, top to bottom."), and I briefly explained what each of those things meant.

Peter and all the other kids just listened as I spoke, staring at the rubric as I read from it. Peter looked particularly thoughtful. When I stopped talking, I waited in silence for a little while because I could tell he was thinking about something. Finally, he asked, "What would I have to do to get into number six?"

I was stunned by how simple his question was. And I couldn't believe that I hadn't posted the rubric in my room, way back in October when we'd gotten those fall reports. I felt so stupid, like I had failed my kids. Here it is, May, and I'm just now having this conversation with them. I decided to kick myself later, and I answered Peter's question. I read from the Stage 6 column in Story Sense: "Story shows a clear beginning, middle, and ending." Peter beamed. "I can do that!" I read through the rest of Stage 6 in Story Sense for him, and then from Stage 5 in Conventions.

When I finished, my quiet little Tessa surprised me by asking softly, "Where am I on there?"

I looked up Tessa's fall results and said, "Last October, you were at Stage 4 in Story Sense and at Stage 4 in Conventions, too." She, too, then asked what she had to do to get to Stage 5. She frowned as I began reading and explaining descriptions from the Conventions list of Stage 5 traits: "May begin to use conventional spelling."

"Spelling is hard for me," she said.

I read on. "Writes left to right, top to bottom; may use spaces between words; may use capital letters and some punctuation correctly." She brightened as I read each one of these, exclaiming each time, "I can do that!"

Certainly, the power of rubrics lies partially in what we do with them as assessors of students' abilities, informing our instruction in response to what they help us to learn; but that power has just as much to do with how rubrics can be used to let students inside the assessment process. Peter's and Tessa's questions about how to make it to the next stage illustrate that power. Their questions demonstrate their lack of concern for perfection; they didn't ask what they'd need to do to reach Stage 8. They simply wanted to know what was next for them. And that, of course, is the whole point of assessment for progressive educators. Can we see—and can we then help our students to see—what is next for them?

The perfection orientation that encourages many teachers, students, and parents to value grades more than they value qualitative information about the child's development (e.g., as a reader, writer, thinker, and collaborator) is a destructive one for the great majority of students (Rogers, 1998). This evaluation orientation diminishes the value of assessment. Further, it reduces instructional feedback to the bottom-line message of how far from perfect our students are. Rogers (1998) illustrated the point in this way. Imagine that after a particularly grueling day at work, you arrive home to find that your partner or spouse has prepared an exquisite meal for you. The ambience is wonderful, complete with soft candlelight, a great bottle of wine, and romantic music. After enjoying the evening together, you turn to him or her and say, "Wow, honey, that was so incredible. I really needed that tonight. Now, I did notice that the vegetables were slightly overcooked, but overall, it was just terrific! You get an A minus!" Clearly, a perfection orientation isn't healthy in any relationship, much less in the ones we have with the children in our care.

Well-defined *standards*, on the other hand, are valuable because of what we can learn about where students are operating relative to them and because they can help us to see what is next for each child to learn. With the perfection orientation that *standardization* encourages, however, we dehumanize learners by prioritizing the standards over the people working toward them. We dehumanize students by seeing them through the standards, rather than the other way around.

Peter's and Tessa's orientation to what was next for them to learn is an empowering one for learners and teachers alike. What it requires from teachers (in addition to a child-centered disposition) is developmental knowledge in the academic/skill areas as well as in children's patterns of social development. No new teacher can be expected to begin her career with this kind of knowledge already in place. Through the use of rubrics that define predictable, developmental stages (typically created by experienced professionals collaborating over a period of years or even decades), the beginning teacher can build this foundational knowledge over time.

Approach #3: Involve students and parents in discussing and setting goals.

Using these kinds of rubrics as one of your principal forms of assessment serves the additional purpose of enabling children and parents to participate with you in the processes of setting learning goals for students and working intelligently toward them. Through knowing about predictable stages of progression in the acquisition of academic skills and in social development, teachers, parents, and students alike are empowered to identify learning goals that are specific enough to be useful. Without the kind of detailed information about developmental stages that such rubrics provide, learning goals are more likely to be stated in overly broad terms, resulting in goal statements that are both ambiguous and useless. (Compare, for example, "I want to be a better writer" with "I want to be able to write strong sentences with powerful verbs.") By thoroughly assessing a student's performance, evaluating which stage of development he is in, and then using the description of the next stage of development to identify and prioritize specific new learning goals, you can help him and his parents to understand what comes next. Better yet, if you have access to *exemplars* (actual samples of what each stage looks like), you can let the student and his parents literally see what he is working toward.

Until now, we have encouraged you to be clear in articulating and defining *your* goals for your students, but this does not accurately reflect our intent. Referring to "your goals" for your students, until now, was simply meant to streamline previous points and maintain focus on them. A learner-centered educator striving to live the ideal of *educere* in her classroom will certainly have her own ideas about appropriate learning goals for the children in her care, but imposing them without involving students and parents in the discussion is a teacher-centered rather than learner-centered approach.

When you first begin working with new students, you lack the information you need for establishing appropriate goals with them and their parents. Your focus must be on gathering enough information to help you to determine students' performance levels or stages in the developmentally defined rubrics you have chosen to use (or which were provided for you by your school or district). Say, for example, that you have decided to use the 6+1 Trait® Writing rubrics (Northwest Regional Education Library, n.d.) as the basis for your writing instruction and assessment. After thoroughly familiarizing yourself with those 6+1 rubrics and using them to score practice papers (examples are available at the Northwest Regional Education Laboratory Web site), you will use the rubrics to assess your own students' writing. After assessing a number of papers from each student in a particular trait, you will be in a position to judge (evaluate) that child's developmental level in that area of writing. Ideally, you will teach students how to use those 6+1 rubrics to rate sample papers and their own writing as well. The power of these rubrics is not only in the insights they provide you as a teacher of writing but also in the opportunities they give you to invite students inside of the assessment process.

By the way, if you have not yet learned about this powerful approach to assessing and teaching writing, we strongly encourage you to seek opportunities for doing so. Rather than treating "writing" as a single skill, the 6+1 traits define seven specific areas to address when teaching students to write: ideas, organization, voice, word choice, sentence fluency, conventions, and presentation. Each of these areas is developmentally defined in its own rubric. A few hours at the Northwest Regional Education Laboratory Web site will orient you to the philosophy and the tools.

After spending the first weeks of the year determining students' performance levels in the skills you are teaching, you can use details from the rubrics or other assessment instruments that you used to help students and their parents to choose a small number of specific, individualized learning goals for each subsequent quarter of the school year. Goal setting does not have to be an overly formal and time-intensive process. During conferences, simply provide students and parents with a copy of the assessment instruments you used that show current levels of performance in each skill area that you're responsible for teaching. Then you can read the descriptions of the next level of performance together, highlighting the specific goals from those descriptors that you, the student, and the parent agree are the most appropriate elements on which to focus. Parents and students can then leave this conference with a good idea of current levels of performance in each area as well as a focused plan that outlines what you will be tackling together in the coming term.

This approach is extremely powerful for helping parents to feel capable as supporters of their children's learning. Many parents wouldn't know where to begin if their child's learning goal was "to become a better writer." With specific, concrete goals established, however, most parents will be able to assist their children's development in specific, well-defined areas—either coming up with strategies on their own or implementing ideas that you suggest.

Finally, note that goals can address aspirations that go beyond content standards. Students may need to learn how to make friends, to gain control of impulsive behaviors, and to grow in social confidence. These kinds of goals are equally deserving of articulation and support.

Approach #4: Be clear about where your instruction is headed before you begin teaching.

At the start of a new unit—whether it is on the Civil War (or civil wars), media literacy, or the concept of balance—be certain that you can name the knowledge and skills that you will be assessing and that you can clearly envision and communicate what success will entail. This approach invites you to create your own assessment instruments and observation routines that are specific to the content, projects, and processes of your particular classroom. It also highlights *clarity* as a fundamental goal of instruction that is directly linked to effective assessment practices. The progressive educator's goal in this context is to help all children to be successful by being extremely clear in communicating the learning goals that will be assessed. These learning goals will usually be specific content-area knowledge and skills, but they can also define relevant social skills like cooperation or collaboration.

A more traditional educator may not consider assessment as a natural and necessary correlate of instruction. While a progressive teacher knows the end goal of instruction before she begins teaching any particular content or process (as well as being able to defend that goal as relevant in the current lives of her students), the more traditional teacher may decide what to assess after her instruction is complete. Her approach to assessing students' knowledge about cell structure, for example, might follow a sequence that goes something like this: (1) have students write definitions for vocabulary words; (2) quiz students on their ability to memorize these unusual, decontextualized words and their definitions; (3) teach a number of lessons about cells, having students complete an equal number of corresponding worksheets; (4) create and administer a test to check on students' ability to complete a cumulative, condensed version of those worksheets from memory; (5) count the number of right and wrong answers each student provided; (6) translate that number of right and wrong answers into a score or letter grade (thereby "evaluating" students' knowledge); (7) return students' tests and review correct answers; (8) record grades; and (9) move on to osmosis. (For her part, Kaia knows this pattern well from having followed it quite a number of times during the first years of her career!)

On the other hand, a progressive approach to assessment would be more likely to follow a "backwards planning" sequence that goes something like this: (1) before beginning to teach, decide what knowledge and skills are most important for students to understand the topic; (2) decide how students would be able to demonstrate those essential learnings, ideally in broad enough terms to allow for a degree of student choice (e.g., create and present a model or poster, form a panel of experts with two or three other students and participate in a Q & A session, or write a report); (3) establish the criteria that will be used for assessing those final projects through rubrics or lists of "quality criteria" (Marlowe & Page, 2005), and either involve students in creating those criteria or make them available before students begin working on their projects; (4) use a variety of instructional strategies to help students learn the knowledge and skills they will need to be successful in meeting the assessment criteria; (5) take notes while observing students as they work, recording details (successes as well as misconceptions/mistakes) that illustrate how they are incorporating new knowledge and developing new skills; (6) use those anecdotal notes to guide subsequent instruction, reinforcing and reteaching concepts and skills, as needed; (7) give students opportunities to assess their own performances and projects, using the established criteria; and (8) use those criteria to give students specific feedback, helping them to see what they learned and have yet to learn.

> When teachers are not able to articulate from the start what the learning goals are and how success in achieving them will be recognized, assessment becomes a game in which students are left to make their best guesses about their teacher's instructional priorities. Eli's story makes the point. His mother, a professor of education, tells her student-teachers his story to help them understand what is at stake on the other side of clarity:
>
> > In third grade, Eli seemed to be doing fine. It wasn't until the next school year that I found out that he had stomachaches every day going to school. At the beginning of fourth grade, he showed me a rubric that his teacher had written for one of his projects, and then he said, "It's so nice to know what I'm supposed to do!" I asked, "Didn't you know what you were supposed to do last year?" He said, "We were supposed to be perfect, but we never knew what perfect was."

When teachers are not explicit about instructional goals, students pay the price. Confusion, frustration, and apathy are logical responses to a situation in which they are left too much alone to figure out what is important enough to pay attention to. This is a more confusing process for students when it involves their performance on qualitatively oriented ("subjective") projects and assessments than on quantitatively oriented ("objective") ones. We prefer the terms *qualitatively oriented assessments* and *quantitatively oriented assessments* to the more usual descriptors of assessments as "subjective" and "objective." Given that even a multiple-choice test is subjective in terms of the teacher's decisions about what items to include and exclude, and in terms of how those test items are worded, we reject the idea that "objective" assessment is possible.

By "qualitatively oriented projects and assessments," we refer to processes, projects, and products that are assessed in terms of the qualities of the student's performance. Qualitative performance rubrics can define a continuum of developmental stages in a particular area, as described in Approach #3, or they can define a continuum of differing levels of quality and sophistication in describing students' performances on specific classroom projects or processes, as will be described in this section. Quantitatively oriented assessments, on the other hand, define achievement in "counting" terms: answers can be counted as either right or wrong, and the essential attributes of the performance are either present or not. Checklists and yes/no/sometimes scales are examples of quantitative performance rubrics.

Both qualitative and quantitative performance rubrics are valuable; the purpose determines the style. Generally speaking, the lower-order thinking processes of Bloom's taxonomy (knowledge and comprehension) are more efficiently assessed via quantitative assessments, while increasingly higher-order processes (application, analysis, synthesis, evaluation) require qualitative means for their expression. Rubrics can assess quantitative, qualitative, or a combination of quantitative and qualitative elements of a performance.

Clarity about the learning goals being assessed is typically easier to achieve on quantitatively oriented rubrics and tests (e.g., true/false, multiple-choice, short-answer tests, checklists); therefore, we will focus discussion of this approach on developing rubrics for the more difficult purpose of achieving clarity in assessing qualitatively oriented performances (e.g., writing an essay, making an oral presentation, cooperating with group members, being a positive community member, being a good teacher).

One reason for you to create a qualitative rubric to assess a particular project, performance, or process (ideally with your students) is to help students to understand the verbs that represent important social or academic processes in your classroom. For example, if you encourage your students to respect each other, not all of them are likely to share a common understanding of what you mean at a deep and operational level. However, if you brainstorm with students ways that they can tell when one person is being respectful of another in the context of your classroom and then use that list of attributes as the basis for creating a community rubric on respect, every student will get the idea. Similarly, if you require a student to compare and contrast selected American wars from the eighteenth to twenty-first centuries, only some students will know what to do; by brainstorming what it means to compare and to contrast, however, and then by using those lists to identify specific steps to follow when comparing and contrasting those wars, every student will have a fairer chance to succeed.

Rubrics that clarify the verbs we use help all students to understand the language of instruction. Encouraging students to reflect on their learning is an admirable goal, but unless they are helped to understand how to reflect, it's an empty one. The idea of teaching the verbs and not only the nouns—that is, teaching the how as well as the what—is one that we attribute to educator Shari Graham (1995), who said, "My students may never again need to interact with what they did in my class—the content. But they will, for the rest of their lives, experience how they did it. The question I must ask of myself is, 'Have I taught them the verbs, and not only the nouns?'"

Creating qualitative rubrics with students is also an effective approach to facilitating community development in a way that genuinely involves them in maintaining their own community norms. If you begin to experience that uneasy feeling that's signaling some kind of problem in your classroom, the first step mentioned in Chapter 1 is to figure out how to name it. Once you have the name of the problem and can describe it, you can engage your students in clarifying and solving it. If the name of the problem is that kids are constantly being nasty to one another, or that they aren't listening actively when other students (or one student in particular) presents work, or that students aren't collaborating effectively in small-group work, you can engage students in creating rubrics to further define, clarify, and productively address the problems. The rubric in the first of these three examples might be called "Being a Positive Community Member," the second "Active Listening," and the third "Small-Group Teamwork." We assess what we value, and we give value to what we assess. Helping students to think through what the verbs mean allows every student a fair chance of being successful in doing them.

Another reason to create a qualitative rubric is to clarify project expectations. If you are going to have a science fair, students need to have guidelines beforehand that define the continuum of quality and sophistication for different kinds of science fair projects. If your kids are going to be reading buddies with younger students, they should go into the experience knowing the kinds of things that an effective reading buddy does compared to a less effective one. If students are going to present research on the history of their community, they need to have clearly defined expectations in hand before they head into the project. When students have the opportunity to use rubrics to shape their work and then to assess their performance with it, they are positioned to be more informed, involved, and invested in their learning.

A critique of rubrics by Marlowe and Page (2005) inspires several important cautions to keep in mind when relying on qualitative rubrics as an assessment strategy:

1. An excessive emphasis on how well students are doing something will tend to undermine their motivation to learn and ultimately impede their performance. Rubrics can be productively used to enhance intrinsic motivation and skill development by

communicating expectations clearly and by engaging students in the process of establishing and owning the performance criteria, but if this kind of tool is used to encourage a perfection orientation instead of a growth orientation, it will have lost its potential as a powerful learner-centered approach.

2. Rubrics that reduce levels of performance to a number promote a quantitative rather than a qualitative approach to communicating what students know and are able to do. This encourages students to focus on grading rather than learning. The most powerful rubrics coach students to understand the progression of sophistication in a given performance, not in attaching a number to a performance level. In other words, the most powerful rubrics are qualitative coaching instruments, not quantitative judging instruments. Students need to be helped away from the perfection orientation that numbers and letter grades promote. Qualitative rubrics can help us to coach kids toward a habit of thoughtful consideration of the choices they make and of their own developmental progression as learners.

3. Rubrics should not be conceived as objective, scientifically accurate measures of students' learning and understanding. We see them as powerful in terms of the challenge they offer teachers to reveal their biases and assessment values, which will inevitably shape constructions of what success means in their classrooms. Qualitative rubrics thus serve to narrow and to focus the subjectivities involved in assessing students' learning, not to eliminate them. When students are able to participate in constructing these value statements, the essential elements of identity and ownership (which have nothing to do with objectivity) are built into the assessment process, promoting students' sense of agency and authority as learners.

While involving students of every age in the creation of rubrics is a good idea whenever possible, you must be familiar with the process yourself before you can lead others in it. Following the suggested steps below, you could create a rough draft of a qualitative coaching rubric by yourself in less than an hour. It may take more time when you first start working on rubrics with students, combining the time you spend in class (no more than 15–20 minutes) and the time you spend alone organizing, polishing the wording, and formatting the rubric (unless you allow a couple of volunteers in your class to take responsibility for this work).

Writing a Qualitative Coaching
Rubric for Class Processes and Projects

Step 1. Name the process or the project that you will be defining in the rubric (e.g., the process of active listening).

Step 2. Project yourself forward in time and imagine that process or project being done spectacularly well. Picture an actual student who you know will be very successful at it and then brainstorm a list of all of the observable things he does that make him good at it. For example, a really great listener gives the speaker culturally appropriate eye contact, asks relevant questions at appropriate times, looks interested, takes notes, sits upright—perhaps even leans slightly toward the speaker, gives the speaker helpful nonverbal feedback (e.g., nodding, smiling, or frowning if confused or puzzled), avoids distractions (passing notes, having side conversations), and demonstrates appreciation appropriately. If you have students who are physically incapable of doing things like sitting upright, seeing, or choosing where their eyes will focus, you have an opportunity to brainstorm with your class a more inclusive set of descriptors. If it is safe in your classroom for students to have different abilities and needs, it will be safe to have them think and talk about the different ways that active listening can be demonstrated. (For the sake of clarity in describing the following steps in the rubric-writing process, we will use the active listening descriptors listed above for typically able students.)

Step 3. Study that list of brainstormed attributes of success, looking for similarities and categories to emerge. Write down all of the categories you can think of, then group the attributes under the three to five category names you like the best—the ones that best represent your (and ideally your students') top priorities. For example, possible categories to use in organizing the attributes of active listening might be facial expressions, body language, and maintaining focus. These category headings, in the jargon of rubrics, are the *traits* that will be assessed by you and by the students. Be sure to limit the number of traits to reflect only the most essential aspects of the process, product, or project you will be assessing with this rubric. A rubric with more than five traits will give you and your students too much to hold in mind while you use the rubric to assess students' (and your) listening skills. Finally, while you're categorizing the brainstormed attributes into these three to five categories, it's okay to delete attributes that aren't priorities and to come up with new ones that occur to you during this process.

Step 4. Write descriptors for each of the traits, defining what success looks like for each of them. Use your brainstormed list of positive attributes to write brief, descriptive sentences or bulleted lists for each trait. For example, the facial expressions trait could be defined in this way: "The student's face is open and interested; he or she gives the speaker appropriate eye contact; the student encourages the speaker by offering helpful nonverbal feedback—nodding, smiling, or frowning if he or she is confused or puzzled." Write a similar descriptor in narrative or bulleted form for each trait. You have now completed defining the advanced end of the continuum for active listening.

Step 5. Now imagine the student who demonstrates extremely poor listening skills that are not attributable to physical ability. Brainstorm a list of the things that this student does, taking care not to write them in overly negative or disparaging terms. For example, this student probably engages in side conversations or passes notes, has an inexpressive face that looks inattentive or bored, rolls eyes, slouches, doesn't look at the speaker, shows appreciation inappropriately or insincerely (e.g., whistles or applauds too loudly), yawns, and makes no apparent effort to understand or engage mentally in the content of what is said. Essentially, you're simply brainstorming opposite attributes from Step 2.

Your rubric will be valuable even if you do not complete Steps 5-9, stopping after defining only the proficient end of the performance continuum. However, we believe it is useful to let students in on the process of defining low-end and average performances; by doing so, they become more conscious of the range of performance categories that you see, and they are helped to internalize value for a high-end performance.

Step 6. Write descriptors for each of the traits you identified in Step 3 (i.e., facial expressions, body language, and maintaining focus) to define the opposite of success, describing what undeveloped listening behaviors look like. In writing a descriptor for the facial expressions trait, for example, you might write: "The student's face may be expressionless, offering the speaker no visible encouragement or feedback; he or she does not give appropriate eye contact; the student may roll his or her eyes, yawn, or show other facial expressions that communicate a lack of engagement and interest. Appreciation for the speaker's work may be inappropriately expressed for the social context (e.g., whistling in a theater) or come across as insincere (e.g., clapping too loudly or with apparent sarcasm)." Write a similar descriptor in narrative or bulleted form for each trait.

The thing to remember when writing descriptions of undeveloped skills is that you do not want to write them in terms that are overly negative or insulting. You will probably have students performing at this level; your assessment efforts should never be overtly discouraging or demeaning. Focus on describing the undeveloped end of the traits in matter-of-fact, observable terms that will help students to understand and to grow. Only if they feel safe, valued, powerful, and capable will they be motivated to change. You have now completed defining the undeveloped end of the continuum for active listening.

Step 7. Think now of the typical in-between student who doesn't stand out as being a particularly good or particularly poor listener. You don't need to brainstorm attributes as you did in Steps 2 and 5; since you have already defined both ends of the continuum, you will draw from both lists to create descriptors of the average listener. The following, for example, describes that middle-range performance for the facial expressions trait of listening: "The student shows a degree of engagement by offering an occasional nod or smile; he or she maintains appropriate eye contact with the speaker periodically, but at other times the student's eyes wander along with his or her apparent attention. Attention to the speaker is not consistent, and appreciation for the student's work may not always be appropriately expressed." This tends to be the most difficult set of descriptors to write. The challenge is to describe the actual, average performance rather than writing obvious in-between descriptions as in, "The student's face is sometimes open and interested; he or she sometimes offers focused eye contact; etc."

Step 8. Decide what you will name each level of performance on this performance continuum. For example, performances can be described as developed, emerging, beginning; home run, double, single; etc. (We like to put the high end of the performance continuum first, to focus students' attention right away on the standard to strive toward.) The thing to keep in mind is that you do not want the name of the undeveloped end of the performance continuum to sound like an insult; if that's where a student is, that's simply where he is. He needs straightforward feedback and encouragement to move into the next stage, not a put-down.

A final note about the levels of performance defined in your rubric: three performance levels will typically provide enough detail to give you enough information for effective assessment, allowing you to differentiate between low, average, and high performances, but it's possible to define more than three levels if greater detail is needed. Keep in mind, though, that the more performance levels you define (e.g., highly developed, developed, emerging, beginning), the more complex the tasks of writing and using the rubric.

Step 9. Format your rubric to look something like Figure 3.1:

Figure 3.1   Listening Rubric

Listening Rubric	Developed	Emerging	Beginning
Facial Expressions	The student's face is open and interested; he or she gives the speaker culturally appropriate eye contact; he or she encourages the speaker by giving facial feedback—nodding, smiling, even frowning if he or she is confused or puzzled.	The student shows a degree of engagement by offering an occasional nod or smile; he or she maintains appropriate eye contact with the speaker periodically, and at other times his or her eyes seem to wander along with his or her attention.	The student's face may be expressionless, offering the speaker no encouragement or feedback; he or she does not offer appropriate eye contact; the student may roll his or her eyes, yawn, or demonstrate other facial expressions that communicate a lack of engagement and interest.
Body Language	Etc.		
Maintaining Focus	Etc.		

Step 10. Use the rubric. Have students use it to self-assess and use it yourself to help focus your observations and to write notes on each student's performance. Always consider a qualitative performance rubric as a draft in progress; as you use it, you and your students will find ways to improve it, to say in ever-clearer ways just what you mean to say when describing various levels of performance.

After you are comfortable with the process of writing rubrics on your own, involve your students in the process. This may take more than one session, initially. Do not put your kids through the entire process in one long sitting; they'll learn to dislike rubrics rather than to see them as powerful opportunities to shape their own experiences in school. The importance of engaging students in this process can be appreciated by considering the different messages that students would receive in the following scenarios.

Scenario 1. You hand students your finished version of a listening rubric and tell them that you will be assessing them with it.

Scenario 2. You describe for students a problem that you're seeing, that students are not listening actively to each other. You ask them to think and talk about why this is a problem, helping them to process internally and understand what is at stake. You go through each of the steps above with your students. You finish organizing students' ideas as you type a draft of that rubric for their review. You let them know that their self-assessments of their own listening skills, using the rubric you created together, will weigh in right alongside of your assessments of their listening skills—and you tell students that the rubric applies to you and every other adult in the room, too.

By involving your students in this approach of clarifying social and academic goals, you will be honoring their need to feel valued and powerful. When basic needs are met—when students know that they are safe, valued, powerful, and capable—they are in a position to want to learn.

Approach #5: Consciously, continuously focus on developing the habits of observation and documentation.

Sarah Lawrence-Lightfoot (2003) described the importance of observation by relating it to the topic of effective parent-teacher conversations:

> Dialogues between parents and teachers are best when they are focused on the specific strengths and capacities of the individual child, providing descriptive evidence of progress or weakness. When parents hear the teacher capture the child that they know, they feel reassured that their child is visible in her classroom—that the teacher actually sees and knows him or her—and they get the message that she really cares. Parents yearn to hear that the teacher appreciates their child, and that is conveyed through a vivid portrayal of his or her life in the classroom, not through platitudinous praise or saccharine sentimentality. (pp. 104–105)

Lawrence-Lightfoot went on to name three skills that teachers need to develop to do what she calls "this subtle and highly individualized work" (2003, p. 105). First, they must develop their observational skills, becoming "students—even connoisseurs—of human behavior." Second, "they must be trained in the skills of record-keeping and documentation. They must develop the daily discipline of note-taking and journal-writing; they must follow their intuitions with careful records that either confirm or challenge their earlier suspicions." And, third, "they must learn to listen—to really hear—the voices and perspectives of parents" (p. 105).

Effective, purposeful observation requires: (1) an assessment focus (i.e., clear social and academic goals that have been identified for groups and for individual students); (2) developmental awareness (i.e., knowledge of where students are and of what is next for them to learn); (3) an intentional, consistent process for observing students and recording notes; and (4) time. Your assessment focus and developmental awareness will derive largely from the rubrics and other assessment instruments you use that define predictable stages of developmental progression as described earlier in this chapter. What remains for this discussion is the need for establishing a regular process for ongoing observation and documentation of what students know and can do.

One of the problems that traditionalists can create for themselves is to make time for observing students simply unavailable. In classrooms where teachers are the doers, where content standardization and classroom management are the instructional priorities, there are few moments in the day when they are not required to be at the center of activity. It's hard to be constantly at the center of activity and simultaneously observe individual students. In learner-centered classrooms, on the other hand, students are the doers. They are engaged in projects; in collaborative activities; and in reading, writing, and creating independently. Effective, purposeful observation of children can happen when students are encouraged and empowered to be independent, when your focus can shift from policing behaviors to observing and guiding them.

This is one of the reasons why community development in the classroom (as opposed to classroom management) must be a priority. Students who believe in the importance of their own community norms, who feel responsible for honoring them, and who know that you have faith in their abilities to do so can release you from the role of sole enforcer and allow you to become an observer. Clearly, this won't happen overnight. You will be spending the first several weeks, perhaps even months, slowly working your way toward increasing student ownership of the classroom environment. Even after most students are able to honor community norms and work independently, there will be problems, slip-ups, mistakes that you and your students will need to address.

You will always need to be vigilant, but you will not always need to be the sole enforcer of classroom rules. You cannot be always at the center of that kind of activity and still have time to observe and document the evidence of your students' knowledge and skills. If your goal is limited to developing your own classroom management skills rather than on developing a community in which everyone is responsible for honoring and maintaining class norms, you will be limited to what you can accomplish from within the confines of that hectic command center that you will have created for yourself.

Time is your most precious resource as a teacher. You can create time for observation and assessment by encouraging students' ownership of and independence in the classroom. Once you have time for observing your students, you'll need to make the most of it. This is where having an intentional, consistent process for observing students and recording notes comes into play. You obviously can't observe everything that each student knows and can do, so you will need to prioritize the academic and social goals that you want to observe and assess. A good place to begin identifying social goals for individual students would be through the community norms—the behavioral ideals that you created with your class. A checklist (that is, a table with all of your students' names written in rows on the left and all of your class norms written in columns across the top) can be an efficient way to see which students need to focus on achieving which social goals. Academic goals can be identified with the help of developmental rubrics, standards, and benchmarks. Once academic and social growth goals are identified (ideally with students and their parents), you can create goal folders—individual assessment maps to focus your efforts in observing and assessing what each student knows and can do.

Keeping track of progress toward those growth areas for 25 to 125 or even more students is the next obvious challenge. Some teachers jot observations on mailing address labels that they later transfer onto students' goal sheets in their folders. A nice benefit of using mailing labels for recording observation notes is that you can print sheets of labels with students' names preprinted on them. For example, Monica prints one sheet per week, with a different child's name on each label on the sheet; this allows her to preprint students' names as well as the date or the number of the school week. She uses this strategy to ensure that by the end of each week, she will have written at least one specific comment or brief anecdote about each of her students. Clearly, though, a teacher who works with the same 25 children each day will be able to record more observations per student than one who sees 125 or more every day.

Another strategy for documenting focused observations is to make a point of observing particular students on particular days of the week (five in each class on Monday, another five on Tuesday, and so on). If you use this approach, you can print sheets of labels with the same student's name on every label, along with the goals that child is currently working toward. Then on Monday, pull the goal sheets of the five students you'll be observing that day, put them on a clipboard, and record your observations of those particular students. Another approach is to make checklists with room for each student's name down the left side of a page and classwide and/or individual goals across the top, leaving room for brief comments in the grid.

A final anecdotal note-taking strategy that we can suggest is to record observations about students during regular periods in the daily schedule (e.g., Author's Chair, Independent Reading, Math Centers). In following this strategy, you would create folders for each of those periods with a few sheets of paper for each student inside, upon which you would write observations about each child's struggles and achievements during those particular times of the day.

Whatever system you adopt, a point to keep in mind is that your purpose is simply to record brief, specific descriptions of observable behaviors; you do not have to interpret them and make sense of everything that you're seeing in the moment. For example: "Feb. 22: Frannie asked if the word *coach* would need to be capitalized when she was writing a story today about Coach Carol in her P.E. journal"; "March 1: Frannie attempted the use of quotation marks to retell a conversation between Coach Carol and herself during class today."

After weeks of observation, several descriptive notes—all focused on a small number of specific social and academic goals—will have accumulated for each of the learners in your care. As time goes by, you will be able to interpret the cumulative picture of what students are showing you and then be able to make informed interpretations and judgments regarding their progress. The details of those notes will provide the basis for your vivid portrayal of each student's life in the classroom that a parent must hear to know that you truly are *their* child's teacher.

Approach #6: Teach students how to create and maintain portfolios of their work.

This strategy will be described in more detail in Chapter 5, "Evaluating and Reporting Student Growth." For the purposes of this chapter on assessing what students know and can do, the relevant point is that portfolios of student work are essential if your goal is to encourage and empower students by allowing them to see evidence of their own growth over time.

Portfolio assessment was a hot topic in education in the 1990s, but it lost steam when educators in various states were unable to demonstrate the reliability and affordability of this approach to authentic assessment. It was also bogged down by conversations that focused largely on ownership issues (e.g., Where would portfolios be stored? How would they be passed on from teacher to teacher, from year to year, and from school to school? Who had the right to decide what items would be included in the portfolio?). Our perspective is that the value of portfolio assessment is both immediate and immense. From this point of view, the child, the teacher, and the parent are the primary benefactors of the process, not future teachers or administrators (although these can be important secondary audiences). The point is not to establish a standardized system of portfolio assessment as an exercise in bureaucracy in which uniform sets of folders follow all students through 13 years of schooling. The point, instead, is to create a manageable, organized, classroom-level system for keeping track of one year's progress so as to make growth visible to the child, to you, and to her parents. That growth, in its visibility, represents what is most valued from that school year in the academic life of the child. The portfolio itself can provide students with their own motivation for continued learning.

We see classroom-level portfolios as a collaborative process between the teacher and the student. Maintaining two kinds of portfolios helps to organize that collaborative process. *Working portfolios,* kept on a quarterly basis, are simply folders to hold accumulations of a particular student's daily work. Working portfolios can be kept in a variety of ways in keeping with your instructional/organizational style (e.g., by content area, by month, or by interdisciplinary units). A single *conference portfolio* (also created anew on a quarterly basis) contains purposefully selected pieces from each of the content-area working portfolios. These pieces are selected by the student, with the teacher's help, because they reflect particular successes or failures relative to the student's learning goals during that quarter of the year. They are accompanied by reflections, written by the student, explaining how the selected work reflects either the achievement or the continuing challenge of a particular learning goal. The conference portfolios, taken together, provide a graphic picture of the learner's achievements and growth over time. Terri Austin's 1994 book, *Changing the View: Student-Led Parent Conferences*, provides a wonderful explanation of how to construct and use conference portfolios.

Approach #7: Share your own growth goals with your students and their parents; invite their feedback on your performance.

By sharing your own growth goals with your students and families and by inviting their helpful critique of your progress toward them, you will be demonstrating the combination of confidence and humility that you hope to encourage in each of your students. You will also be modeling the idea that vulnerability and strength are two sides of the same coin. By reflecting publicly on how progress toward those goals is coming along, you will be able to show your students a couple of important things: that it is through reflection that learning is realized and that you, too, are a learner.

SUMMARY

In this chapter, we explored strategies for observing and assessing what students know and can do. We discussed the following approaches for developing and refining your skills of observation and assessment:

- *Enjoy the challenge of becoming a skilled observer and assessor of your students' knowledge and abilities.* One of the things that makes a teacher great is his ability to figure out what underlies his students' behaviors and beliefs.
- *Let students inside of the assessment process.* The whole point of assessment for progressive educators is to be able to see—and then to help our students to see—what is next for them.

- *Involve students and parents in discussing and setting goals.* Knowing about predictable stages of progression in the acquisition of academic skills and in social development empowers teachers, parents, and students to identify specific learning goals for each child.
- *Be clear about where your instruction is headed before you begin teaching.* The progressive educator's goal in this context is to help all children to be successful by being extremely clear in communicating to students the learning goals that will be assessed.
- *Consciously, continuously focus on developing the habits of observation and documentation.* An intentional, consistent process for observing students and recording notes is essential to your ability to see where your students are and what is next for them to learn.
- *Teach students how to create and maintain portfolios of their work.* Create a manageable, organized, classroom-level system for keeping track of one year's progress for each student so as to make growth visible to the child and to her parents.
- *Share your own growth goals with your students and their parents; invite their feedback on your performance.* In doing this, you will be demonstrating the combination of confidence and humility that you hope to encourage in each of your students.

4

Planning Instruction

When the topic of interdisciplinary unit planning came up for the first time in Sandra's student-teaching seminar, she laughed out loud. Then she shared the connection she'd just made with her five-year-old son.

Robert had started kindergarten that fall. His teacher was absolutely wonderful; she was warm, enthusiastic, and clearly devoted to her students. Before the school year had even begun, she introduced the teddy bear unit she had planned as a way to welcome her students to school. In the middle of August, she mailed teddy bear cards to each of the children on her class list, sharing some information about herself and about the kinds of things they could look forward to experiencing in her class. She told them about a traveling teddy bear who had his own backpack and who could go home with different students on different days. When the first day of school came, the children's names were waiting for them at their tables, printed neatly on teddy bear nameplates; they had teddy bear cutouts to color and teddy bear graham crackers to eat at snack time. The day was filled with stories, songs, and activities, and in one way or another, they all involved teddy bears.

Like many kindergarten moms, Sandra had left her little boy's classroom that morning in tears; her baby was growing up. At the end of the day, she was eager to hear how his first day in school had gone. He was tired when she picked him up at the classroom door, and she waited until they got to the car before finally asking him, "So what did you think? How was your first day in kindergarten, Robert?" In his five-year-old voice (complete with lisp and lazy r), Robert said, "Oh, it was all right." Curious and a little let down by his lack of enthusiasm, Sandra probed further. "What did you get to do today?"

Robert sighed as he summarized his experience thus far of school. "It was okay, Mom. But they sure are into teddy bears over there!"

In telling this story, Sandra made a point of recognizing that the teddy bear unit couldn't have been more well-intentioned or thoroughly and creatively planned, and she sincerely *appreciated Robert's teacher for her obvious desire to make her son feel welcome and excited about his first year in school. The connection that she made with this story, though, months after Robert's first day of school, is that instructional units need to offer students of all ages the chance to engage with real questions and relevant substance. As harsh as it may sound, the problem with "teddy bear units" is that the connection between fun, creative activities and substantive content is not always clear. Unless those content connections are relevant and obvious, the only message clearly sent through interdisciplinary or thematic units is that some of us teacher types are remarkably fond of a pretty short list of topics. In the context of thinking about instructional planning, it is useful to empathize with Robert, imagining what was going through his head as he tried to make sense of his new discovery about kindergarten. "They sure are into teddy bears over there!"*

Effective instructional planning is an incredibly complex challenge, even for experienced educators. Luckily, it's a fun one, too, for teachers who tend to enjoy complex challenges. It requires consideration of a great number of educational concepts and processes, and those who are beginners need time and support as they continually work to develop their knowledge and skills in these many areas. We encourage new teachers in particular to expect frustration and productive confusion, to value and learn from mistakes, and to extend the same kind of patience and kindness to yourself throughout this learning curve as you would for any other learner in your care.

Effective instructional planning requires in-depth *knowledge* of (1) the concepts and skills taught (i.e., the subject matter); (2) students' current knowledge, skill levels, and interests (which explains why we intentionally positioned this chapter between the chapters on assessment and evaluation); (3) accommodations and modifications required by individual students for them to be successful; (4) the developmental progression of knowledge and skills in each content area taught; (5) grade-level standards and benchmarks; and (6) instructional resources available.

Effective instructional planning also requires highly sophisticated *skills* in (1) lifelong reading, learning, and reflecting, particularly in one's content areas; (2) assessing students' current levels of content area knowledge and skills; (3) unit planning; (4) lesson planning; (5) implementing appropriate accommodations and modifications for individual students; and (6) effectively using available resources.

The breadth and depth of concepts and practices that are entailed in planning instruction make this chapter particularly ambitious. What will follow is simply our best shot at addressing the many layers involved. Readers are encouraged to focus on implementing strategies that resonate with them one at a time. Teaching is hard enough without putting ourselves through the perfectionist's tendency to want to implement everything immediately!

Before we begin, it is necessary to return for a moment to consider again the Continuum of Educational Thought described in the Introduction. We believe that it is possible, even probable, that any given teacher's philosophy can travel a range of educational thought, depending upon which topic is under consideration (e.g., curriculum, accountability, standardization, motivation, or classroom/school environment). Our philosophies of education are complex and personal. As we wrestle to resolve the tensions that can exist between our ideals and the realities we're living, it is not unusual for educators to feel pulled between traditional and progressive ideals. The five continua of educational thought in the Introduction can be useful because they give us a way to understand and express those internal tensions. In doing so, they can help us to become more conscious, to be able to explain better the reasons why we make the choices that we do in our schools and classrooms.

We want to be clear, particularly in the case of this chapter on instructional planning, that we are not writing this text from the perspective of radical progressivism. In the realms of curriculum and accountability, our thinking tends more toward a moderate position on the progressive side of our Continuum of Educational Thought. This reality reflects the uneasy tension that we feel between our progressive ideals and our pragmatic compulsions. From one perspective, it would be wonderfully freeing if district and state level standards didn't exist: teachers and students could explore anything and everything in pursuit of the development of thoughtful habits of mind, the internalization of broad and deep content knowledge, and the sophistication of critical skills in every content area. At the same time, we also believe that district and/or state standards are helpful in providing guidance and structural support to teachers, particularly to those who are new to the profession.

This is why our approach to instructional planning reflects a more moderate than far-left position on our Continuum of Educational Thought. It is not necessarily an easy place to occupy; the realms of curriculum and accountability, more than any other, indicate the juncture where our ideals and realities collide. Even so, we find the process of instructional planning to be intensely rewarding—perhaps *because* of the complexity it presents.

We believe that standards can be addressed in a great variety of ways, through an equally great variety of questions, topics of study, and learning activities. It is possible, when instructional planning is approached critically and creatively, to address standards through topics of student interest and social importance. In this way, standards can be made to work for you and your students. They are useful when you know them well enough to be able to point to the specific standards that led you to supplement your social studies textbook's treatment of Columbus' "discovery" of the New World with *Rethinking Columbus* (Bigelow & Peterson, 1991), for example. They are useful because the job description of a public school teacher is partially written in the language of standards. Therefore, the political work of ensuring that Native American students, in this example, can see their historical and current realities fairly represented in a curriculum that acknowledges the role of racism, past and present, in defining those realities is not a challenge that an individual teacher must undertake alone. When we know our standards well, we can connect to them in ways that serve the democratic ideals of progressive education. This is the practical challenge for every teacher who wishes to fit the school to the child in today's public school context: to align standards to student needs rather than the other way around and, in doing so, to honor the idea of standards insofar as they serve the learners in our care.

Finally, while instructional planning necessarily must address knowledge and skill development, this chapter will be primarily devoted to facilitating students' exploration of art, social studies, science, and health content. Countless books are devoted to skills-based instruction (e.g., reading, writing, math), which is beyond the scope of this text.

FROM THEORY TO PRACTICE: STRATEGIES FOR PLANNING INSTRUCTION

Approach #1: Get to know your curriculum guidelines.

To be able to help your students to become more *skillful* in each content area, you must be familiar with the developmental progression of those skills. (As described in Chapter 3, professionally created rubrics and other materials defining developmental skills progression are essential for this purpose.) To guide your students in becoming more *knowledgeable* in each content area, it's helpful to begin by becoming familiar with your district's or state's adopted curriculum documents and/or content standards. As a new teacher, then—whether you are new to the profession, to a grade level, or to a particular course—an initial goal must be to get to know your curriculum guidelines. You can then use these guidelines as a starting point for finding out what your students already know.

In addition to learning about the curriculum you're responsible for teaching, another goal is to develop a large-picture perspective on these content area guidelines for the entire grade level. Educators in elementary schools will do this naturally, as they are typically responsible for teaching their students in most subject areas. It is important for middle school and high school teachers to bring this big-picture perspective into focus, too. Even though an eighth-grade science teacher is not responsible for the social studies curriculum, for example, she can find interdisciplinary connections only if she is familiar with the full picture of her students' experience of the eighth grade—and to our way of thinking about instructional planning, interdisciplinary connections are what it's all about. Of course that eighth-grade science teacher will be most deeply familiar with the science curriculum, but by at least reading through curricula in each of the other content areas, she will be able to find concepts that will link the disciplines together. If she is familiar with the science curriculum alone, she will have only scratched the surface in finding ways for her students to learn about and connect with science and their world.

Interdisciplinary connections can be identified conceptually and topically. Abstract concepts (e.g., energy, balance, and leadership/ followership) as well as more concrete topics (e.g., the civil rights movement, engines, and water) offer opportunities for elementary, middle school, and high school teachers alike to work with colleagues in their schools, creating units that demonstrate an important idea for students: that the disciplines are simply different perspectives or lenses that we can use to understand ourselves and the world around us (Jacobs, 1989, 2002). They allow us to explore important topics and concepts—like energy, the civil rights movement, courageous leadership/followership, and water—from a variety of perspectives.

While the individual lens of science can be a powerful means for learning about engines, for example, that single perspective cannot provide the breadth or depth of connections that many lenses or points of view can. Imagine how much richer students' experiences and understandings will be if they have opportunities to extend their scientific study of this concrete topic into the conceptual realm, examining the concept of an engine through the lenses of social studies, health, art, math, language, and physical education.

Stop here, if you will, and really consider that last sentence. Think about the topics, questions, resources, and learning activities that come to mind when you consider teaching a unit on engines from a "social studies" perspective and then from each of the other disciplinary perspectives. Better yet, do this out loud in conversation with someone else and experience the fun of instructional planning! This experience of finding connections and achieving a greater depth of understanding is the essential justification for interdisciplinary teaching and learning.

Another reason to cultivate an interdisciplinary style of teaching is that interdisciplinary study brings coherence and unity to what most students currently experience as a terribly fragmented approach to education. Heidi Hayes Jacobs (1989), whose model for unit planning provided the basis for the approach we will describe, explained this fragmentation problem with an analogy. Imagine that someone has handed you a textbook with the table of contents and index ripped out. The book will still contain all of its original content information, but you will have no access to its organizational framework. That, she says, is what we routinely do to students. We give them a number of unrelated experiences every day and expect them to find the connections and make sense of it all.

Compounding the fragmentation problem that Jacobs described is the sheer number of concepts that American students, in particular, must often try to synthesize on their own. According to Willard Daggett (1998), founder of the International Center for Leadership in Education, for example, the number of math and science topics that students are required to learn has grown steadily in the United States over the past few decades. At the same time, the number of math and science topics has been shrinking in some of the countries that have fared better in the Trends in International Math and Science Study (TIMMS) conducted by the International Association for the Evaluation of Educational Achievement. Daggett reported that in the first TIMMS report of 1978, American students grappled with 57 math topics in their eighth-grade year, while Japanese eighth graders dealt with 32 topics. In the second TIMMS report of 1986, the number of topics rose to 67 for American students and decreased to 23 for their Japanese counterparts. In the third TIMMS report of 1997, that number rose farther still for American eighth graders, to 78, while it shrank to 17 in Japan.

Similarly, in describing the problem of "unfocused textbooks" in the United States, Schmidt, McKnight, and Raizen (1997) wrote that "the average U.S. science textbook at the fourth, eighth, and twelfth grade has between 50 and 65 topics; by contrast Japan has 5 to 15″ (Unfocused Textbooks section, ¶2). This breadth of content coverage is simply too much for our students to be able to make sense of on their own.

Through the process of becoming familiar with an entire grade level's worth of curriculum, even if you are not an elementary teacher, you will find the large, unifying concepts that your students need help to see—the essential connections linking the disciplines that can provide much-needed focus for students' experiences in school. Your goal is to help the learners in your care to understand that the educational system—like any system, whether it is the human body or a government with three branches—is made up of essential, interdependent components. Students can then appreciate the role and the power of each discipline, not as merely another subject that they are required to take but as different avenues for making sense of the world. With a systemic perspective on education, they can entertain such questions as what might happen to the overall well-being of a system when one of its essential components (like art or music, for example) is allowed to wither away.

Approach #2: Develop and teach interdisciplinary units.

From a moderate progressive perspective, the ultimate goal is to involve your students in interdisciplinary planning, after you have become confident enough in the process to be able to facilitate their participation. The steps described below are written for teachers who are working on developing that sense of confidence in their skills as planners of interdisciplinary units. Note that while these steps are described in a sequence that is logical to us, we do not mean to suggest a lockstep approach to creating interdisciplinary units. Readers may find another sequence or alternate steps in the process more useful or better aligned with their own planning style.

Acknowledgments: The process for creating interdisciplinary units that we describe below is based on Heidi Hayes Jacobs' Interdisciplinary Concept Model (1989), and we gratefully acknowledge her work in this field. Modifications to her design have their roots in a number of workshops that Kaia facilitated in Kodiak, Alaska, from 1995 to 1997 and in methods courses that she taught at the University of New Mexico from 1999 to 2005 and at California State University Channel Islands from 2006 to the present. Hundreds of preservice and beginning teachers have contributed to the modifications of the Jacobs model reflected below. Finally, the unit topic described in Step 1, "Animals in the Sky," was developed by Judy Reagan, Dale Hagen, and Kaia Tollefson.

Step 1: Identify the topic for your unit. You can begin looking for powerful unit topics in your district's curricula or the state's content standards for your grade. Your social studies, science, health, and arts curricula are particularly great places to find ideas for interdisciplinary units. Where language arts and math curricula usually tend to be more focused on skill development, the subjects of social studies, science, health, and the arts are typically more concerned with content knowledge. Think of these curricula as vehicles for giving relevance to skills development in the three R's of reading, writing, and arithmetic. This way of thinking places essential language and math skills in service to the study of important ideas and topics rather than being the primary goals of instruction themselves.

If you haven't already done so, carefully read your social studies, science, health, art, music, physical education, math, and language arts curricula. Make a list of all of the main topics outlined in each area. Then take your time and look for connections between these lists of curricular goals. For example, "animals" and "light" were two major science topics taught at the third grade in one school district; and in social studies, third graders were to be able to "demonstrate ways in which language, stories, folktales, music, and art are expressions of and an influence on behaviors in particular cultures" (Albuquerque Public Schools, 2001, Grade 3: Social Studies: Scope and Sequence). The question for creative interdisciplinary planning, then, is this: What unifying concept might exist to link the topics of (1) animals; (2) light; and (3) the influence of language, stories, folktales, music, and art on behaviors in particular cultures? A unit on constellations is one possibility that would provide a framework for integrating the exploration of all three of these big ideas.

Imagine the difference it will make to the third graders who are in two different classrooms. In one, the students study separate units on animals, light, and the influence of language and art on individual and cultural identity. In the other, they engage in an interdisciplinary unit on constellations. The name of this unit is "Animals in the Sky." These students learn about reflected and refracted light by studying the stars, they use constellations as a launching place for the study of animals, and they learn how early human beings explained their lives and their world with myths about the origin of the constellations and the animals they represent. The questions they explore in this unit are provocative, and they invite interdisciplinary exploration:

1. *Why do people need a "starry, starry night"?* The topics that can be taught through this question are many, including the characteristics of a star, identification of "animal" constellations, light, navigation, beauty, music, art, myths, and legends.

2. *What do animals in the sky look like, act like, and live like on the earth?* Topics this question offers for study, for example, include identification of constellations during different seasons, classification of constellations, classification of animals, the food chain, and the needs and survival methods of animals.

3. *How are you like a star?* This question offers the opportunity to appreciate the words *star* and *constellations* in broader terms. To what "constellations" does each of us belong? What does the word constellation really mean, and why is it an important concept?

The process of discovering large, unifying themes that cross disciplinary lines is an essential step. Take the time to be very methodical in identifying the big ideas you will be teaching in each curricular area. Take the time to be creative in finding possible connections between these topics and skills. You have completed the first step in the process when you've identified a tentative theme and/or title for your unit.

Step 2: Brainstorm connections between your tentative unit topic and each content area. You have just read each curricular document for your grade level in each of the content areas—including those that you may not be directly responsible for teaching. Specific activities that you could do with your students in studying your tentative unit topic should be fresh in your mind. This step is about writing those ideas down.

Use a graphic organizer like the one pictured in Figure 4.1 to record connections between your unit topic and each curricular area in brief but specific detail. In other words, under each discipline heading on your brainstorming web (language arts, math, science, social studies, visual and performing arts, health, physical education), record your ideas for specific activities, books, field trips, guest speakers, games, experiments, songs, questions, vocabulary words, Web sites, and any other kinds of ideas you can think of that connect to the topic you'll be studying. The more specific you are in recording your ideas during the brainstorming stage, the easier it will be for you to complete the next steps in the process. Resist the urge to access the Internet for ideas at this point. First tap your own creative ideas and connections so that you can develop a sense of kinship with the topic. We have seen beginning teachers lose themselves in the avalanche of great ideas that are available online; some don't recover and are unable to organize that avalanche into a coherent and content-rich unit of study.

When you are finished with the first draft of your brainstorming web, take a minute to consider how much richer your connections to the unit topic are because you approached the topic from all disciplinary perspectives rather than solely through science or language arts or any other single subject. Jacobs advocated doing this step eventually with students, involving them in all steps of unit planning, once you are familiar enough with the process yourself to facilitate kids' participation in it. When students have the chance to brainstorm connections between the disciplines and a particular topic, Jacobs said, they come to appreciate the disciplines as perspectives or lenses rather than merely as vague and arbitrary blocks of time that fragment their days.

Figure 4.1   Graphic Organizer: Brainstorming Web

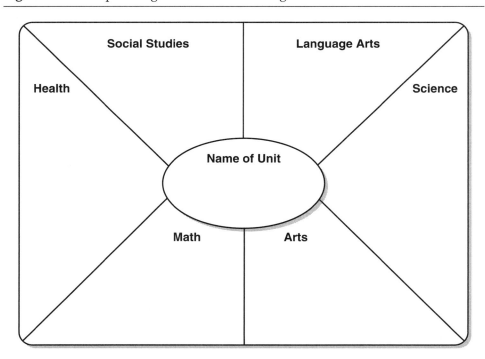

You can facilitate students' participation in brainstorming content-area connections by framing the disciplines in terms of people who work in those areas. "What kinds of things might a writer do if he were studying 'Animals in the Sky'? How about a mathematician? A scientist?" For older students, offer more specialized roles to represent each content area. "What project might a documentary film-maker tackle to show others something about the 'Animals in the Sky'? What would a sociologist or an anthropologist do to explore this topic?"

Whether you brainstorm alone, with colleagues, or with your students, the goal at first is to achieve quantity. You can find connections and refine your ideas later. For now, work to fill every bit of white space in your brainstorming web. Even if you will be teaching the unit on your own, getting a colleague or friend to help with the brainstorming will give you more breadth and depth in your ideas for how you could teach the unit. Brainstorming with others makes the process more fun, more productive, and more creative.

Step 3: Begin to search for instructional materials. If you were able to brainstorm a great number of content-rich, feasible, and creative connections between your tentative unit topic and at least several of the content areas, chances are good that you have found a unit topic that is worth developing further. What remains to be seen is whether adequate resources are available for actually teaching it.

In this step, you will finalize the choice of your unit topic (or discover that you need to choose a new one) by beginning your search for high-quality, credible resources. Start a reference list for the resources you find, following the guidelines below:

- This list should be topic specific, not age or grade specific. Great resources are often easily adaptable to different grade levels, and excellent ones are worth the trouble.
- Be sure to consider different learning styles and intelligences in your compilation of materials. Include a wide variety of media: books, CDs, DVDs, Web sites, guest speakers, field trips, local/state/federal agencies, artwork, music, etc.
- Include in your list only those items which you deem to be high-quality, credible resources. Don't include everything you find; just list the resources that you think are genuinely worthy of your students' time and attention as well as your own.
- Differentiate your references by noting whether they are instructional resources (things you can use with students) or background

materials (reference information for deepening your own content knowledge).

- Annotate your references. Provide a concise summary (one or two sentences) of each item on your list. Taking the time to do this now will save you time down the road. This reference list will grow every year that you teach the unit; you will want to have a way to remember what each item on your list is. Annotations for community resources can include contact names, telephone numbers, e-mail addresses, and other relevant information that will give you a starting point in future years as you check into accessing them again.
- Work for breadth (many different categories of resources—books, Web sites, music, field trips, games, etc.) and depth (as many resources as possible within each category). Your goal is to have more options available than you will possibly be able to use. Having breadth and depth will allow you flexibility, putting you in position to pick and choose which resources you want to use as you develop the unit and use it from year to year rather than being locked into only a few meager options.

Your immediate goal at this point, before proceeding to Step 4, is to determine whether enough resources exist to warrant further development of your topic. You don't have to complete the resource list right now; you only have to make sure that enough resources are out there to allow you and your students to have an in-depth experience in studying this topic. Your search for high-quality, credible resources will continue throughout the process of creating the unit, even extending into future years as you continue to use and modify it.

Step 4: Narrow the focus of your unit by identifying your primary purposes for teaching it. In Step 1, you brainstormed so many activities in each content area that you would need an entire semester or more to complete them all. You went for quantity in your brainstorming web, exhausting your ideas in the search for as many interdisciplinary connections on that topic as possible. Now it's time to funnel it down by identifying your instructional priorities for the unit. In this step, you will focus your topic by identifying your most important reasons for teaching this particular unit. You will start by examining your brainstorming web and naming all of the themes that you see emerging from it—all of the big ideas that your students could possibly explore while studying the unit's topic. Then you'll prioritize your top three to five themes—those large, unifying concepts that reach across the disciplines. The following guidelines will help you to identify those themes that will ultimately represent your instructional priorities for the unit:

- Study your brainstorming web while considering this question: At the end of this unit, what are the things that I want my students to know and be able to do specifically because of their participation in it?
- Make a list of all of the ideas that occur to you in response to that question. Each of these big ideas, or themes, must be large enough to allow room for more than one disciplinary perspective (i.e., language arts, science, social studies, math, art) in exploring it. Note that according to Jacobs, if a particular discipline doesn't contribute powerfully to the study of your unit's topic, it's better to leave it out and teach that subject separately at another time in the day than to force weak connections. Her wonderfully practical approach is one of the reasons that we started with her model.
- When you have exhausted your brainstorming web for themes, go through your list and identify the three or so most important ones—the ones that represent the essential learnings that you believe are at the heart of this unit. Note that the number of themes you choose as your instructional priorities for the unit must reflect the amount of time you have available for the unit as a whole. For a four- to six-week unit, three themes are typically plenty. It's okay to have more or less than that, but keep the goals of *depth* and *coherence* in mind as you plan for the amount of time available. Too many themes in too short of a time will cause incoherence and prohibit you and your students from engaging deeply with the topic.
- Each of your final themes will eventually be expressed in the form of an essential question. These essential questions will represent the teaching and learning priorities for your interdisciplinary unit. Writing essential questions will be addressed in Step 8 below.
- Double-check your final choice of themes. When taken together, will they (1) provide a place for each of your top instructional priorities for the unit; and (2) lend themselves to learning activities that span the full range of thinking processes (i.e., Bloom's taxonomy: knowledge, comprehension, application, analysis, synthesis, evaluation)? Does each theme define a distinct instructional goal, or do they overlap?

At this point, you have (1) identified your unit topic; (2) brainstormed connections between that topic and curricular goals in each content area; (3) ensured that adequate resources are available for teaching it; and (4) established the unit's main themes, which will serve as prioritized avenues of inquiry into your unit's topic. These themes represent your top priorities for teaching and learning this unit. A final check on your themes will occur in the next step.

Step 5: Categorize learning activities from your brainstorming web by theme and by discipline. At this point, your initial planning papers probably look extremely messy—a good sign that you've chosen a rich topic for your unit. You began bringing focus to the mess in the preceding step, when you purposefully chose a small number of instructional priorities for the unit out of the many possibilities that you initially brainstormed. When you look at that brainstorming web, though, you still have a visual mess on your hands—even though you *may* be able to feel small sprouts of coherence beginning to grow in your mind. If it feels as though you're swimming in the mud of too many ideas, though, that's okay. Try to be patient and trust the process.

The purposes of this step, in which you will organize the ideas from your brainstorming web under the headings of the themes you identified in the last step are (1) to provide a visual sense of order to your work thus far, (2) to check again that the themes you chose are really the ones you want, and (3) to get a visual picture of which disciplinary perspectives (science, social studies, etc.) will be the most useful for exploring each of the themes. You can expect that individual themes will lend themselves more to some disciplines than others. You may find through completing this step that you've discovered no powerful connections between a certain discipline and any of your themes. Again, it's okay to make the decision *at this time* to leave out that discipline. Avoid omitting a subject area from the unit prior to this step, however; doing so too soon can keep you from seeing potentially powerful connections that you may not have expected to find.

Create a table like the one in Table 4.1. Then move ideas from your brainstorming web to the table, categorizing those brainstormed learning activities by theme and by subject area. Expect to find that not all of your brainstormed ideas will "fit" under your chosen themes and that you will come up with more ideas for great learning activities that weren't on your brainstorming web. Also, you may find during this step that your themes are too similar to each other, overlapping too much and making the categorization of brainstormed ideas difficult. Revise your choice of themes/instructional priorities as needed, ensuring that each one represents a distinct avenue of inquiry.

Table 4.1   Learning Activities Categorized by Theme and by Discipline

Theme #1:

Social Studies	Science	Language Arts	Math	Visual/ Perf. Arts	Health/ P.E.

Theme #2:

Social Studies	Science	Language Arts	Math	Visual/ Perf. Arts	Health/ P.E.

Theme #3:

Social Studies	Science	Language Arts	Math	Visual/ Perf. Arts	Health/ P.E.

Step 6: Identify the content standards in each discipline that are clearly (not peripherally) related to the unit themes/instructional priorities you have chosen. This step is about keeping track of the content standards in each of the disciplines that you will be addressing through this interdisciplinary unit. Metaphorically, this unit will serve as the vehicle for carrying those particular content standards to your students. In documenting this (perhaps by making a list of the relevant standards by theme/instructional priority or by highlighting them or color coding them on a printout of your grade-level content standards—however you want to organize the task), you will be taking a step toward authoring the terms of accountability in your own practice.

Step 7: Create a "unit frame" of Bloom's taxonomy activity matrices. A unit frame is a summary of your themes, essential questions, and learning activities, all organized according to Bloom's taxonomy, with one page per theme. Investing time in creating a unit frame will bring returns for weeks to come. When you have completed your Bloom's taxonomy matrices of learning activities (Figure 4.2), you will have completed the bulk of your instructional planning for as many weeks as the unit will last. This is important not only from a time-saving perspective (invest it now to save it later) but also for the even more important reason that by putting forth the time and effort now in planning a four- to six-week unit, you will know where you're headed and why the journey is worthwhile to begin with. We teachers have the privilege and the rather daunting responsibility of deciding how to best spend children's lives while they are at school—and to help them to become increasingly able to make good decisions about how to spend their own life's time, in and out of school. Investing the time and the effort it takes to be clear about what we're teaching and why we're teaching it is simply a great way for us to honor our students' life-times. They're further honored when we are confident enough in the process to invite students to participate in some of these unit-planning steps.

To review: At this point, you have a clearly defined unit topic, clearly stated themes for exploring it, and a beginning picture of how each subject area will contribute to the exploration of those themes. What you do not have is any assurance that your students will get to exercise any more of their brains than the parts that can remember facts and processes (knowledge), understand them (comprehension), and apply them (application). This is where many of us who teach often fail our kids. We typically give our students all kinds of opportunities to exercise these essential lower-end thinking skills but don't offer consistent opportunities for them to enjoy the challenge of exercising their brains in more complex ways. Their access to academic activities requiring higher-order skills is typically limited, meaning that they seldom get to make sense of a big concept or mechanism by examining its parts and figuring out how those parts work together to form the whole (analysis), to design or create a completely original work by applying what they have learned through a number of different experiences (synthesis), or to develop and apply original standards for judging the quality or value of something (evaluation). This step is designed to ensure that your unit will invite students to exercise their brains along the full range of thinking processes, using an organizing framework like the one in Figure 4.2.

You will be creating a separate activity matrix like the one in Figure 4.2 for each of your themes. Your challenge in this step is to translate the learning activities from Step 5, which were categorized by theme and

Figure 4.2   Unit Frame: Bloom's Taxonomy Activity Matrix

Bloom's Taxonomy Activity Matrix					

Unit Title: _____ Grade Level(s): _____ Created by: _____

Theme/Instructional Priority # _____:

_____

Essential Question for This Theme:

_____

Circle learning activities that you will use as opportunities to formally assess students' knowledge and/or skills.

Knowledge	Comprehension	Application	Analysis	Synthesis	Evaluation

by subject area, into the language of Bloom's taxonomy. Follow these guidelines in completing your unit frame:

- Create blank Bloom's taxonomy activity matrices, one for each of your themes.

- List the activities that correspond with the first theme on your Bloom's taxonomy matrix #1. Activities for the second theme will go on matrix #2, and those for the third on matrix #3.
- Place each learning activity at the highest level of thought that students will exercise in completing it. For example, asking students to "explain the significance of the 'Gettysburg Address' in a one-page essay" presumes (1) their knowledge of that speech, (2) their comprehension of it in the context of everything else that they know about the Civil War, (3) their ability to apply their writing skills and their knowledge about the Civil War, (4) their ability to analyze the role of that particular speech in the context of the larger whole of that war, so that they can successfully (5) *synthesize* what they know and can do in the form of an original essay. That activity would therefore be categorized under the highest level of thinking accessed, synthesis. Note that students' quality of higher-order thinking will be wholly dependent upon the quality and depth of what they have achieved at the lower-order end of the scale. Knowledge and comprehension are no less important than synthesis and evaluation; indeed, they make the complex thinking processes possible.
- Take care to write activities in terms of what *students* will be doing. Each learning activity can be very briefly described, and *each one must begin with a verb that you can literally watch a student do.* This is important, because you can assess and evaluate only what you can observe. A learning activity that requires students to "understand the water cycle" is pointless, since you cannot watch a student understand something. You can, however, observe whether or not those students can accurately "illustrate the water cycle."
- You may not be able to come up with activities for each level of Bloom's taxonomy for each theme. This is to be expected. Some of your themes and associated essential questions may lend themselves more to the knowledge and comprehension end of the continuum, while others invite more opportunity for synthesis and evaluation. It is important, however, to make sure that when taken together, your activity matrices as a whole will provide students with access to the full continuum of thinking processes.
- Guard against the temptation to list activities just because they're fun. Each learning activity you describe must contribute *significantly* to your students' ability to answer one or more of the essential questions. Selecting activities is a matter of wisely using your most valuable resource—your students' time.

- The next step describes the process of writing essential questions, one for each of the large themes that represent your instructional priorities for the unit. As you create your unit frame by listing learning activities on these Bloom's taxonomy activity matrices, be sure to include a "culminating activity" on one or more of your matrices. Culminating activities are designed to allow you to see if each student is able to answer those large essential questions.
- The unit frame is valuable not only for providing *instructional* direction and focus. It also offers you a wealth of ideas for *assessing* your students' knowledge and skills. Every single activity listed on those matrices is a potential assessment opportunity, since each one begins with a verb that represents important knowledge and skills that students will need to achieve the essential learning goals of the unit. Which activities lend themselves to paper-and-pencil assessments? Which to a culminating performance assessment, utilizing a qualitative rubric that you create (ideally with your students)? Identify the learning activities that you will formally assess and then create your assessment instruments before you begin the activities. Share the assessment instruments with students either at the beginning of the unit or the particular activity; if possible, involve your students in their creation. If you can, provide students with accompanying samples of what "success" on that particular activity or project might look like.

Step 8: Write an essential question for each of your themes. Your students may never see the names of your instructional priorities for the units, that is, the themes around which you created your unit frame in the previous section. They will see the essential questions that you write to represent those priorities in a provocative and essentially kid-oriented way. We teachers are constantly asking questions in our classrooms, but our unfortunate tendency is to wade in the shallow end of the inquiry pool. Right-answer questions thoroughly dominate our collective habits of inquiry, a reality that encourages students to believe that being educated is about knowing answers to other people's closed-ended questions. A steady stream of right-answer questions that lasts for 13 years will also bore the shoes off many kids—and many teachers, too.

The purpose of this step is to find engaging, creative, compelling reasons for kids to care about this unit that you've worked so hard to create. If your essential questions provoke and intrigue *you,* chances are good that they'll do the same for your students. Singer and songwriter John Prine gave us the ultimate mind-set to cultivate in the process of writing essential questions: "A question ain't a question if you know the answer, too." Real questions are ones that you want to explore right along with your kids.

Heidi Hayes Jacobs (1997) described the power of essential questions in terms of their ability to communicate the importance of studying unifying questions rather than fragmented subjects in school. Imagine that you are a high school English teacher and that you and two colleagues in other disciplines have gotten together to create an interdisciplinary unit. The three of you have identified a unit topic, brainstormed connections to your content areas, named your collective instructional priorities for the unit, created your unit frame of Bloom's taxonomy activity matrices together, and written your essential questions. Then each of you posts that list of essential questions in your separate classrooms. As students go through their day, moving from your class to science, and from science to social studies, they'll see those same questions again and again, posted on the walls of their various classrooms. And they'll start to think about that unit topic in larger terms. They'll begin to wonder about the connections. They'll learn to see education in an intriguing new way.

When you have your unit's essential questions posted in your classroom, Jacobs said, you have a built-in mechanism for keeping kids' focus on what they are learning instead of on what they are doing. Imagine having those questions on your wall, teaching one of the lessons from the unit frame, and then asking students to defend their opinion as to which of those essential questions the lesson's activities helped them to answer. Such a habit on your part will encourage students to look beyond the immediacy of the current activity and to focus instead on why they are doing it.

Well-written essential questions, then, serve a number of purposes: (1) they represent the teaching and learning priorities of the unit to your students, (2) they focus students' attention on the disciplines as the means for education rather than the ends, (3) they provoke students' interest in a topic by approaching it through interesting and open-ended inquiry and the exercise of higher-order thinking skills, and (4) they invite students and teachers to explore important questions together. In writing essential questions, the challenge is a creative one as you work to find just the right way to represent your instructional priorities for the unit.

As you work to translate your themes into essential questions, the most important guideline follows from the Prine quote above, which is important enough to bear repeating: "A question ain't a question if you know the answer, too." The essential guideline in writing essential questions, then, is to craft questions that provoke *you*. You will know when you've hit on a good question by how it makes you feel and by what your own mind wants to do with it. When you finally come up with a question that perfectly captures the intent of one of your themes, and when that question is so well written and obviously important that it makes you want to put your pencil down and start talking about it with someone, you've found a good contender for representing that instructional priority. Other guidelines include the following:

- Use easily understandable sentences and words. Students should be able to understand the question immediately and see that it is important and answerable.
- Remember that each question represents an entire avenue of inquiry for studying the unit's topic. A question that is answerable in a single day or through a small number of learning activities is not substantial enough.
- Questions should be listed in a logical sequence that you are able to explain. When you get to Step 8 below, however, note that it is not necessary for students to complete all activities associated with essential question #1 before moving on to exploring question #2 or #3. It is possible for you and your students to approach the unit by studying one question at a time, but it's not necessary.

Once you have come up with a great question for each one of your unit themes, complete your Bloom's taxonomy activity matrices by writing your essential questions on them.

Step 9: Sequence the activities in your Bloom's taxonomy activity matrices. The purpose of creating a sequence chart (Table 4.2) is to help you to imagine your unit as a whole, flowing smoothly from activity to activity and from day to day. By listing your learning activities in the order in which you will teach them, you will be more able to imagine that flow and identify any "holes" that might exist in your unit. Keep in mind the idea that since your unit includes most, if not all subject areas, you will typically be listing a number of activities per day.

Table 4.2   Sequence Chart

Day #	Name of Activity/Lesson	Essential Question #

Conclusion. A complete interdisciplinary unit plan represents a number of highly significant accomplishments. With a clear instructional focus now charted for the next four to six weeks, you and your students can enjoy a sense of coherence, confidence, and flow—from day to day and from week to week. Secondly, with instructional priorities clearly defined through the Bloom's taxonomy activities matrices, your opportunities for formally assessing students' simple and complex knowledge and skills are also well defined. This definition gives you—and your students—the opportunity to create formal assessment instruments before you teach the unit, empowering you and the learners in your care with a clear vision of what success will entail. Finally, with a plan in hand for engaging students in questions that matter and for giving them access to activities that require higher-order thinking, you will be in position to teach them how to learn. You can let students in on the secret: anyone with a good question and an equally good plan for pursuing it can teach themselves whatever they want to know.

Approach #3: Create lesson plans for purposeful teaching and learning.

Each learning activity listed in your Bloom's taxonomy activity matrices can be developed into its own lesson plan. What follows, then, are reasons and guidelines for lesson planning. We lean on Madelaine Hunter's work in identifying and defining consistent elements of good lesson plans, reflecting again a moderate/centrist perspective on instructional planning.

In our experience with preservice teachers, we have found that most are reluctant lesson planners. The requirement that they must submit a plan before being able to do any of their practice teaching with children (and to do so in time to allow cooperating teachers to suggest revisions before teaching the lesson) is not a popular one. At best, there tends to be a sense of resignation when it comes to writing lesson plans; rarely is genuine interest evident. This reluctance may reflect the possibility that student teachers don't see lesson planning as "real" teachers' real work. After all, they go side-by-side through every day with their mentor teachers, and the only formal lesson plans they are likely to see during the course of a semester are their own. They may not understand that all good teachers are lesson planners—that over the years, the process becomes more fluent, more internal, until eventually a form of shorthand for writing plans is developed.

While writing lesson plans for most teachers is probably located on the thin side of the continuum of deeply engaging and *intrinsically* motivating instructional activities, we believe that the process offers a perfect example of an activity that promotes *identified* motivation (Deci & Ryan as cited in Sheldon & Biddle, 1998, p. 167) for educators: that is, while the behavior itself isn't overly enjoyable in its own right, it can be motivating nonetheless for those who internalize its value and who, therefore, choose lesson planning as something they care about.

We believe that the planning process must be explicitly developed and demonstrated. There must be proof that teachers can design a lesson that is meaningfully learner centered by being purposeful, coherent, clear, appropriately challenging, well organized, open to student input and choice, and relevant in students' current lives. In other words, to earn the privilege of deciding how children will spend their life-times in school (and potentially out of school, on homework), as teachers we must be able to *show* that we get the big picture and can organize the details accordingly. This isn't to suggest that a lesson plan must be thoroughly scripted and rigidly followed. Sometimes the most powerful learning moments come from having the flexibility to modify or even scrap a plan altogether when students take a lesson in a new and productive direction. Rather, lesson plans demonstrate our *preparedness* to teach a well-conceived lesson.

Why write lesson plans? Lesson planning is an essential skill that must be developed for a number of reasons:

- to develop and to practice the habit of reflective, purposeful teaching;
- to demonstrate the ability to create content-rich lessons that have genuine relevance in students' lives;
- to develop organizational skills and the ability to help children to spend their time in school effectively, thoughtfully, and as independently as possible (which includes being able to work cooperatively with others without requiring constant adult intervention); and
- to articulate goals, objectives, and assessment strategies *before* presenting lessons to students (both you and they should be clear about where you are going with the lesson, why it is important, and how it fits into the bigger picture of the students' lives).

When are lesson plans necessary? While we see lesson planning as an essential skill, we also recognize that requirements for them can be overdone. Real life in an elementary classroom, for example, is that dozens of lessons are taught every week. Writing a detailed lesson plan for every activity is not only not feasible, it's just not the most productive way to spend precious planning time. Therefore, we suggest the following guidelines for determining when a full-blown lesson plan is necessary:

- Write a lesson plan for each of the "large" lessons in your week, when new skills and concepts are introduced.
- For daily routines, write one lesson plan rather than a new one each day. However, that master lesson plan for a recurring event—e.g., author's chair, read-aloud, morning meeting—should be modified periodically to reflect the changing focus and objectives as students' skills and knowledge evolve.

How to write a lesson plan. How do you know how much to write? When it comes to lesson plan length and level of detail, you're striving for balance. Write too much, and it's not user-friendly; write too little, and it's not descriptive enough to be useful. Our general guideline is to write with just enough detail so that another teacher could pick up your plan, quickly understand the lesson's purpose and the instructional processes described, and teach the lesson as you envisioned it. Suggested lesson plan components and guiding questions to help with their development follow.

Lesson Plan Development

HEADING

Date:

Teacher Name:

Grade Level(s):

Subject(s):

Topic/Concept:

Estimated Time Required:

Content Standards Addressed: (Be selective here. Don't list every peripherally related standard, just the few that are clearly and directly related.)

GOAL(S), OBJECTIVES, MATERIALS

Goal(s): What are the large purposes for this lesson? How does this lesson fit into the big picture of the students' education? Limit your goals so that you and your students will be able to hold just one or two large purposes in mind as you work your way through the lesson. An important point to note is that your goals for the lesson and your plan for debriefing it should be purposefully linked. Clarifying your goals at the beginning will allow students to process the lesson's impact more purposefully when they debrief it with you.

    1.

    2.

Learning Outcomes: What are the specific, *observable* things that students will be helped to do because of their participation in this particular lesson? By naming observable outcomes (via action verbs), you will be focusing your instruction and identifying assessment opportunities. An important point to note here is that your anticipated outcomes for the lesson and your plan for assessing those outcomes should be intentionally linked. Clarifying your outcomes at the beginning will allow you to assess your students' achievements more purposefully.

From a moderate-progressive perspective, learning outcomes should be open enough to offer opportunities for students to have meaningful input and to make important choices about *how* they will demonstrate their learning, when possible. For example, "design an activity for teaching younger students about the earth's hemispheres" allows for student choice and creativity versus the closed-ended outcome of "identify the earth's hemispheres on a globe." Learning outcomes can begin with the phrase "If I teach this lesson well, students will be helped to . . ." This phrasing, in contrast to the more typical opening phrase of learning outcomes, "Students will be able to . . . ," communicates shared responsibility for students' success. It is also intended to offer a less absolute, less standardized way of thinking about learning outcomes. It is not reasonable to expect all students to achieve the same learning outcomes in the same time frame, no matter how well we teach; but by naming the outcomes we are working toward, we can bring our responsibilities to each of the learners in our care into better focus. Again, severely limit the number of specific learning outcomes for the lesson so that you and your students can truly focus on them.

    1.

    2.

    etc.

Materials: What items will you and the students need for this lesson?

Instructional Materials/Quantity:

    1.

    2.

    etc.

Student Materials/Quantity:

    1.

    2.

    etc.

PROCEDURE/METHODS

Be specific enough so that a reader can picture exactly what you and your students are doing during every phase of the lesson but be brief enough so that the document is useful. General guideline: Could a capable substitute teacher read your lesson plan in 10–15 minutes and then be able to teach it?

Introduction: Briefly describe your "focusing event." How will you provoke students' minds?

Development: Sequence of instruction/modeling/explanation/activities. A suggestion to help with user-friendliness: don't write in paragraph form. Use bullets or numbered lists to describe the steps. Focus on ensuring that the reader can picture the teacher's and/or students' actions in each step.

    1.

    2.

    etc.

Practice: Describe any guided activities you might use to help students work toward achieving learning outcomes for the lesson. (How will students get to practice using what they learned while you're still there to support them?) Further, describe any independent activities you may assign that will allow you to see individual students' progress toward those learning outcomes.

Modifications: How will you need to modify/differentiate instruction, the environment, activities, and/or assignments for specific students? Include consideration for students in your classroom who do not have an Individual Education Plan (IEP) but who require modifications to be successful.

Checking for Understanding: How will you check to make sure students understand how to proceed in small-group work or on their own?

Debrief: How will you bring the lesson to a close? Again, note that your overall goal(s) for the lesson should come back into play here. How will you help students to see the lesson in relationship to the big picture purpose(s) you were aiming for?

ASSESSMENT AND TEACHER REFLECTIONS

Assessment: What method(s) will you use to assess, formally and informally, the effectiveness of your instruction? While your overall goals for this lesson should have come into play in the previous step of debriefing it with students, now the focus is on revisiting the learning outcomes that you identified for this lesson. How can you tell if you were successful in helping students to achieve the outcomes you identified for the lesson? What formal and/or informal strategies will you use to learn about each student's progress toward those learning outcomes? Did any unanticipated outcomes emerge? How will you record what you learn through your assessment efforts?

Reflections: How did the lesson go? What specific evidence from students supports that opinion? What worked especially well? What would you change if you were to teach it again? Taking the time to reflect in writing about how the lesson went will deepen your own sense of purpose in your teaching, and it will give you valuable insight in future years. If you teach the same lesson again, you will have ideas about how to modify it to make it more successful.

Approach #4: Create a year-long curriculum map.

This crucial step in "mapping the big picture" (Jacobs, 1997) is not as daunting as it may sound. You have already studied your curriculum in detail to find interdisciplinary connections for your unit. You have already made lists of the big ideas in each subject area, so you know the topics that other educators in your district or state have recommended that you teach at your grade level. You have looked at those lists of big ideas before, from the four- to six-week perspective of an individual unit. Now spend some time thinking about how those large concepts might fit together over the course of a school year.

Make a copy of your district calendar, and on it, mark the starting and ending dates of each quarter or semester, inservice days, student-parent-teacher conferences, and holidays. Eventually, you will also be labeling this calendar with the names of units or major topics that you will teach throughout the year. To do this, you will need to work toward developing a coherent picture of the many topics of content knowledge and skills you are responsible for teaching. Begin by thinking of all of those topics as pieces of a jigsaw puzzle, each of which will fit somewhere within the linear frame of your district calendar. As you survey the frame and all of those puzzle pieces, there are just two things for you to consider in constructing your year-long curriculum map: interdisciplinary connections and sequence.

Interdisciplinary connections are obviously easier to consider if you are an elementary teacher responsible for most subject area instruction, since you can do much of the connection-hunting alone. Still, in elementary schools where specialists may teach things like art, music, and physical education, classroom teachers can coordinate units/topics with the teachers of those pull-out programs. If you are a middle or high school teacher who shares students with colleagues in other disciplines, you can work with them to figure out which of the big ideas in your disciplines fit together. These big-idea connections form the basis of potential units to be developed.

A caution to keep in mind, though, is that creating and teaching an interdisciplinary unit, particularly if you're working with other teachers, obviously takes a lot of time and effort. If you can create and implement just one or two new interdisciplinary units a year, before long you'll have a wealth of ideas and resources that can serve as an increasingly well-developed starting point for your work with future classes.

Sequencing the curriculum is just a matter of figuring out which set of big ideas—that is, which unit, topic, or set of interdisciplinary connections—should come first in the year and then which should come second, third, fourth, and so on. In determining the logical order for presenting content, consider things like seasonal connections and accessibility of resources. When you have fitted the parts of your curricular jigsaw into its calendar frame, create a map of your academic year by labeling your school calendar with the names of units/topics. With this visual representation of your curriculum drafted, you will have given yourself and your students the mental gift of a coherent plan for the year. You will undoubtedly be revising that map as the year progresses and as student interests unfold, but with a general sense of direction established from the beginning you will be more able to wrap your mind around the complexity of instructional planning.

Approach #5: Use learning centers to give students opportunities to practice working independently on the content and skills they are currently developing.

Whether you call them "centers," "stations," or "corners," the idea is to have areas of the room set up with all of the supplies and learning materials needed for kids to practice using what they have learned. This needn't be as spatially demanding as it may sound; centers can be stored in large tubs that come out only during center time. Centers provide opportunities for students to become more skillful, more accurate, more thoughtful, and more creative because they are being given time to practice using the skills and content knowledge they have learned.

It is common for teachers who are new at using centers to become frustrated when students cannot work independently at them. If students cannot be productively engaged on their own in a particular center activity, this simply means that they may need more support in a more structured setting with that particular content or skill. In fact, one of the most significant benefits of using centers is that they can give you the time you need to do exactly this—to provide individual or small-group instruction for children who are not yet able to be successful in the centers that other students can engage independently. Another important benefit is that they allow you time to observe students using their academic knowledge and skills in authentic settings. If you are disciplined about observing individual students during center time, reviewing particular students' work as they are producing it, and recording anecdotal evidence about what each student knows and is able to do, you will be able to build accountability measures for centers into real time (avoiding at least some of the need to spend your evenings and weekends reviewing the paper trail that documents your students' learning achievements).

Centers can be organized around a single discipline, giving students opportunities in different centers to practice math skills, for example, at differentiated performance levels (see Tomlinson, 1999). They can also be organized by different subject areas. Following are just a few ideas for implementing the latter approach.

In a Writing Center, students can create a mailing center and write letters to classmates, to family members, to characters in the historical fiction book you're reading aloud to the class, to the editor of the school or town newspaper, to the principal, and to guest speakers or field trip hosts. They can work together or alone to write stories, poems, and plays. They can write articles for a class newspaper. They can create illustrations to go with stories that they write or that they dictate into a tape recorder.

In a Social Studies Center, students can ask and explore questions of social significance to their classroom/school/community (e.g., How can we find out if bullying is a problem at our school?), creating questionnaires, surveys, or interview questions for classmates, school personnel, or community members. They can write letters to each other as if they were the historical figures they have studied. They can create two- and three-dimensional maps of the classroom, school, or neighborhood. They can research and rewrite a particular event in history from a perspective that they believe was not adequately or fairly represented in their textbook. Historical, biographical, and autobiographical books can be recorded on tape so that students who have difficulty reading can have access to difficult texts and complex ideas.

In a Science Center, students can explore the topic they are currently studying by exploring the "realia" that it involves. For example, if the class is studying the five senses, students can write descriptions of their experiences with tasting, smelling, touching, hearing, and seeing a variety of objects; if they are studying rocks and minerals, students can compare, contrast, weigh, draw, and label them. They can practice each step of the scientific method, either with an experiment that you provide or by designing and conducting their own. They can analyze discarded appliances, dismantling them to see the parts within.

In a Math Center, students may develop and write solutions to problems posed online (e.g., Nrich, at http://nrich.maths.org/public/, publishes child-authored solutions). They may write in their math journal about investigations underway. They may work at assigned stations on skill-building exercises designed with varying abilities in mind. They may spend time at one center for a week, investigating a complex problem, documenting trials, and communicating results.

In a Listening Center, students can listen to books on tape. They can preview the afternoon's reading selection in science or social studies by listening to an audiotape that you, a parent volunteer, or a student has recorded. They can listen to language learning tapes, quietly practicing phrases in Spanish, English, etc. They can record themselves reading a passage or short book and compare/contrast current readings with recordings they made a month/semester/year ago.

In an Art Center, students can create original works and explore various media that you make available to them. They could watch short video clips about various visual artists and then experiment with that artist's style. They can read about what was happening in the art world during the period they are studying in social studies. They can write original reviews of movies, songs, television shows, and works of art, stating their opinions and defending them by explaining the standards they used to guide their judgment.

Center time can vary in length and can be more or less structured depending upon the goals you have for your students. Some teachers allow students free choice during center time every day; others create a rotation system to ensure that during the course of a week, all students have engaged in each of the centers for a certain amount of time. In addition to giving kids time to practice applying the specific knowledge and skills they have learned, centers naturally allow for differentiation while giving children opportunities to make significant choices about how they want to spend at least a part of their time during the school day.

SUMMARY

This chapter considered the complex process of planning instruction. We presented the following approaches to effective instructional planning:

- *Get to know your curriculum.* To be able to help your students acquire the content knowledge that you are responsible for teaching, you must be familiar with your district's or state's suggested or required curriculum.
- *Develop and teach interdisciplinary units.* An interdisciplinary approach to teaching and learning brings coherence and unity to what most students currently experience as a fragmented approach to education.
- *Create lesson plans for purposeful teaching and learning.* Lesson planning enables you to practice the habit of purposeful, conscious teaching and to create content-rich lessons with genuine purpose and relevance in students' lives.
- *Create a year-long curriculum map.* With a visual representation of your curriculum drafted, you will have given yourself and your students the mental gift of a coherent plan for the year.
- *Create new learning centers every month or so to give students chances to practice working independently on the content and skills they are currently developing.* Centers should provide opportunities for students to become more skillful, more accurate, more thoughtful, and more creative using the skills and content knowledge they have learned in more structured settings.

5

Evaluating and Reporting Student Growth

"In dealing with students, we have to realize that only 25%–30% of them are happy," said Dr. William Glasser (1998b), a psychiatrist with decades of experience in working with kids. "These students come to school with good relationships as their foundation. They reach out to us quickly and easily, and we respond quickly and easily. They do the work we ask them to. But," he said, referencing the Effective Schools Conference at which he'd been invited to deliver this keynote address, "we're not at this conference because of them. We're here because of the other 70%."

Glasser knows about "the other 70%." At one time, he worked in a reform school for 400 teenage girls, kids who had done everything wrong in their previous schools "from mayhem to murder." These girls didn't misbehave in the reform school, though, and Glasser asked them why. Their response was simple: "Dr. Glasser, we don't fail here." When you did the work in the reform school, you got credit for it, they explained.

"When we fail students, they don't get happier. They don't work harder," observed Glasser. "So why do we fail students? We fail them because it's the 'right' thing to do. We don't do so because we believe for a moment that it will help them or improve their learning. We don't do so out of the belief that there is a shred of evidence, anywhere, that supports the effectiveness of grading. We do so because we're supposed to."

Evaluating and reporting student growth, from a student-centered perspective, necessarily empowers rather than labels the learner. Lawrence Kutner (1991), child psychologist *and author, asked, "Do your children view themselves as successes or failures? Are they being encouraged to be inquisitive or passive? Are they afraid to challenge authority and to question assumptions? Do they feel comfortable adapting to change? Are they easily discouraged if they cannot arrive at a solution to a problem? The answers to those questions will give you a better appraisal of their education than any list of courses, grades, or test scores." (p. 117)*

When it comes to evaluating and reporting student growth, most students, parents, and teachers are likely to agree that letter grades (A, B, C, D, F) tell us what we need to know about a student's academic performance. Primary teachers and progressively minded educators and parents may be among the few people in all of society who question that idea. Well trained to accept the apparent objectivity of letter grades (which are usually based on seemingly indisputable numerical data), most students, parents, and even teachers do not consider the stunning subjectivity of the process—much less the hidden values, questions, and power relations that letter grades represent. The everyday, unremarkable practice of grading continues—not because grades are educationally beneficial but "because we are supposed to," as Glasser said. As a result, the practice has remained largely unexamined by the great majority of people who are directly impacted by it.

Even so, for reasons we will later explain, we do not advocate here for abolishing letter grades. Progressively oriented educators who have attempted to do away with grading (in favor of providing students and parents with qualitative feedback about academic progress) have typically been met with rejection by the general public. Everyone has been to school; everyone knows how it's supposed to work. Grades serve as a cherished form of shorthand for a number of institutional functions. They serve to communicate educational priorities, define systemic power relations, mark progress toward students' (and their parents') academic goals, and provide scorecards for gatekeepers in higher education and the job market. When the recognition of this integral relationship of grading with so many institutional functions is coupled with an understanding of the common assumptions about grades that many people share, it is possible, even easy, to understand why challenges to this traditional practice of symbolizing students' achievements with a letter or a number are often unsuccessful.

COMMON ASSUMPTIONS ABOUT GRADES

In his work as an educational consultant, Spence Rogers (1995) invited his audiences to identify what they believe are the major purposes of grades. Typically, groups responded with the following ideas:

- Grades provide means for evaluating students' overall academic performance.
- Grades allow students to be effectively ranked and sorted.
- Grades communicate information about students' content-area achievements to the student and parent.
- Grades are a means of holding teachers and schools accountable to the public.
- Grades provide teachers with information with which they can inform their instruction.
- Grades serve as gatekeepers, as qualifiers for other programs and institutions.
- Grades motivate students.

This list is very similar to a list of four grading purposes identified by W. L. Wrinkle sixty years ago. In his 1947 text, *Improving Marking and Reporting Practices in Elementary and Secondary Schools,* he wrote that grades serve administrative, guidance, information, and motivation/discipline functions. What is interesting about these two lists is that they represent common assumptions about the usefulness of grading to which people have clung for decades—despite research findings dating back to 1912 that have consistently challenged the validity and worth of each one.

A BRIEF HISTORY OF GRADING

It is extraordinary to consider how tenaciously we have clung to our beliefs about grades in light of what the history of grading reveals. In the telling of this story, it is important to distinguish between terms. *Grading* is an evaluative function. It refers to the practice of providing a numerical or letter symbol to summarize a student's level of achievement on a particular task or for a given period of time in a particular subject. *Evaluating* is the making of judgments regarding the quantity or quality of a student's performance, progress, or achievement. *Assessing* is the collecting of information—the observations, in whatever form, that show what the student knows and is able to do.

Since the days of the first academy during Plato's time, students have been assessed. For many centuries, the purpose of educational assessment was primarily formative: teachers' observations and examinations merely provided information about what the student knew so that they could determine what was next for him to learn. Summative evaluation of students—that is, the practice of assigning a single numeric or letter value to represent achievement—is a very recent development in the history of education. In fact, the practice is just a little over 100 years old (Guskey, 1996). This is a rather remarkable perspective: the system we've come to view with such a degree of faith that the average person now rarely questions its existence is only a century old—a very recent development in the 2,400 year history of formal education in the western hemisphere.

It didn't take long for criticism of grades to surface. The grading system we know today was born in this country between 1870 and 1910, when public high schools were quickly multiplying. In 1912, the first serious challenge to the practice of grading was issued. In two consecutive studies, researchers Daniel Starch and Edward Charles Elliott powerfully demonstrated the unreliability of grades (Starch & Elliott, 1912, 1913; as cited in Guskey, 1996, p. 15). In the first, 142 teachers from different schools graded the same two freshman English papers using a 100-point scale; a score of 75 was considered a passing grade. One paper received scores that ranged from 64 to 98, a 34-point spread; the other's ranged from 50 to 97, a 47-point spread. Obviously, the teachers scoring these papers valued different things, and their grading practices showed it. Because response to the study was critical, with objectors noting that good writing is a highly subjective judgment, the two researchers conducted a second study in 1913. This time, 138 teachers from different schools graded the same two geometry papers. Scores on one ranged from 28 to 95. With a 67-point spread, this geometry paper yielded an even greater rating discrepancy.

Since the Starch and Elliott project, a number of researchers have reported related findings. Teachers take different things into account when assigning grades (Bennett, 1993; Brookhart, 1994; Guskey, 1994; Kohn, 1994; Nottingham, 1988; Spear, 1997; Sprouse, 1994). Correctness, showing or failing to show work, difficulty of the assignment, students' perceived ability levels, how a class performed overall, perceived effort, spelling and other forms of mechanical correctness may all be considered in varying degrees of importance by different teachers—depending upon the individual instructor's values. Personal traits such as handwriting and personality have also been shown to influence grades. Some teachers offer opportunities for "extra credit," allowing students to raise their grades by presumably doing more of the same caliber of work. Clearly, the case against the reliability and objectivity of grades has been made and verified, beginning with that first landmark illustration by Starch and Elliott.

EVALUATION AS GRADING: CRITIQUING TRADITIONAL PURPOSES OF LETTER GRADES

Consider again the list of grading purposes generated by Rogers' audiences. The first four of these common justifications for grades (italicized below) are challenged on the grounds of Starch and Elliott's more than ninety-year-old findings:

1. *Grades provide means for evaluating students' overall academic performance.*

2. *Grades allow students to be effectively ranked and sorted.*

3. *Grades communicate information about students' content-area achievements to the student and parent.*

4. *Grades are a means of holding teachers and schools accountable to the public.*

5. Grades provide teachers with information with which they can inform their instruction.

6. Grades serve as gatekeepers, as qualifiers for other programs and institutions.

7. Grades motivate students.

Certainly, the first of these assumptions (that grades provide means for evaluating students' overall academic performance) is challenged. How can performance be reliably evaluated over time if the rating standards are variable and the grading practices subjective? As for the second (that grades allow students to be effectively ranked and sorted), students can surely be compared with each other and reliably ranked within an individual classroom, although we obviously question the educational benefit of doing so. But what if a student is moved into another teacher's class or transferred to another school? In view of what research tells us about grading, the reliability of one teacher's judgment is meaningless in the context of another teacher's classroom.

The usefulness of grade point averages as a valid means for sorting and ranking students is inherently suspect.

The validity of the third assumption (that grades communicate information about students' content-area achievements to the student and parent) is also questionable. If an A means something different to any number of different teachers, and if "achievement" is variably defined in terms of the qualities or characteristics that individual educators value, grades cannot be said to communicate reliable information to students and parents except in particular cases—when individual teachers are explicit about their grading standards and procedures. Assumption number four (grades are a means of holding teachers and schools accountable to the public) is also unfounded; accountability implies a known standard against which measurements are made and through which they have meaning.

Of seven purposes commonly cited as justification for grading, then, the validity of the first four is immediately cast in serious doubt by research that has been available for almost a century. Research findings aside, we would suggest that anyone who has experienced the traditional grading system—either as a student or as a teacher—can confirm these findings of inter- and intrarater unreliability at a personal level.

With the validity of the first four of the most common justifications for grading seriously compromised by research described thus far, three remain for our consideration:

5. Grades provide teachers with information with which they can inform their instruction.

6. Grades serve as gatekeepers, as qualifiers for other programs and institutions.

7. Grades motivate students.

Justification number five, that the practice of grading informs teaching, represents simply a confusion in terms. Assessment practices certainly do provide the teacher with needed information so that he can know what is next for students to learn. But what *instructional* purpose is served by grading—that is, by placing a number or a letter at the top of students' papers? Even if the instructional value is claimed to be for other teachers, for those who will teach the same students in future years, previously described research indicating the lack of agreement among teachers when it comes to grading dispels the idea that grades are reliable enough to serve instructional purposes. We can dispose of rationale number five, then, with the argument that it is not the act of grading but rather the essential processes of thoughtful assessment that inform subsequent teaching decisions.

And so we are left with the two most compelling arguments on behalf of grading: that colleges require them (number six) and that students are motivated by them (number seven).

Proponents of the need for grades are fond of the argument that grades are needed for gatekeeping purposes in higher education. The tone of this argument is often reluctant, apt to be phrased along the lines of, "I don't like grading, either, but as long as colleges use high school grades as one of the criteria for admission, our hands are tied." Although this justification is harder to dispel, a couple of points can nonetheless be lodged against it.

First, there is ample room to doubt the truth of the blanket claim that colleges require grades. Going as far back as 1973, only a small percentage of the nation's two- and four-year colleges have indicated that grades or rank in class were an absolute necessity for admission (Curwin, 1976, p. 143). Also, while high school grades are certainly taken into consideration by college admissions officers, they are not the only deciding factor. Other factors like SAT scores, recommendations, essays, leadership, and extracurricular activities weigh heavily in admissions decisions. Finally, a trend of recent decades has been that there are typically more freshman college seats available than people to fill them (Daggett, 1993). While it is true that competition for positions in the more prestigious colleges and universities is fierce and that GPA typically plays a significant role in that competition, it does not follow that grades are required for access to all institutions of higher learning. With recruitment offices actively seeking candidates to fill freshman seats, it is untrue that *most* colleges would refuse to accept students on the sole basis of their high school GPA.

The GPA argument, then, appears to serve only elite students in elite schools very well—but even then, the argument falters. Some of the most prestigious universities in the United States, including Notre Dame, Harvard, and Stanford, are specifically interested in students who have been homeschooled and who therefore have no GPA (McCusker, 2002). Admissions officers at these universities cite high SAT scores, the benefits of diverse backgrounds and experiences, and "intellectual vitality" (¶9) as predictors of these students' academic success in exclusive schools. From this perspective, rationalizing letter grades as an absolute necessity for college admission is unsound, leaving ample room to doubt the need to formally rate K–12 student's academic performances quite so incessantly.

A second point similarly challenges the fairness of a grading system that is rationalized for all on behalf of the few. Only 28% of Americans aged 25 and older have earned a four-year college degree (U.S. Census Bureau, 2005). This fact, coupled with research suggesting that grades are genuinely motivating for only 20%–25% of all students (Rogers, 1995) must surely yield the conclusion that our current evaluation system is intentionally designed to serve the academically and often socioeconomically elite. Letter grades may serve many of the college-bound well, but it does not follow that this system effectively serves the learning needs of the majority of our students, who are not college-bound or who are not genuinely motivated by letter grades. Martin Seligman's (1991) work in cognitive psychology contributes to this argument from another perspective. In his opinion, the traditional view of achievement needs overhauling because it fails to address students' *feelings* about learning:

> Our workplaces and our schools operate on the conventional assumption that success results from a combination of talent and desire. When failure occurs it is because either talent or desire is missing. *But failure can also occur when talent and desire are present in abundance but optimism is missing* [italics added]. (p. 13)

The introduction of Seligman's theme of optimism introduces to this discussion the essential role of the affective domain as a critical variable in the realm of learning achievement. The long-term value of teachers' and students' work together is greatly determined by the teacher's ability to strike a balance in addressing students' cognitive and affective needs. As psychologist Lawrence Kutner (1991) explained, "Children learn and remember at least as much from the context of the classroom as from the content of the coursework. . . . It is the emotions of the classroom that leave the most lasting and important marks" (p. 177). Arthur Combs, who has been called the father of humanistic education (Caine, 2004), would have agreed. Combs (1976) described the role of emotion in learning in this way:

> It is necessary to understand that all learning is affective and that affect must be understood in terms of relevance. Education must be affective or there will be none at all. If learning is understood as the personal discovery of meaning, then motivation becomes an internal matter having to do with people's beliefs, attitudes, feelings, values, hopes, desires, and

the like. Whatever happens in the classroom must be under-stood in these terms. (p. 7)

Combs' thirty-year-old position, that "education must be affective or there will be none at all," is powerfully reinforced by recent research on the functioning of the human brain (Caine & Caine, 1997; Jensen, 1995, 1998; Kotulak, 1997; Sylwester, 1995; Wolfe, 2001; Zull, 2002).

And so we come to address the last—in no way the least—of ratio-nales for using letter grades to represent students' academic achieve-ments. Assumption number seven states that grades are necessary to motivate students. Children and young adults will not apply them-selves in school, so the logic goes, unless they are made to work for grades. The logic of behaviorism, however, is consistently refuted in social cognitive research (Deci and Ryan, 1996; Hatter, 1978; Ryan and Deci, 2000; Vansteenkiste, Simons, Lens, Sheldon, & Deci, 2004). Rogers (1998) explained,

> Every study I know of from the last twenty years indicates the same thing. Extrinsic motivators lower performance over time. They work in the short term. Kids who are more focused on external motivators continually ask questions like, "How much is it worth?" Their focus is not on learning.

While it is therefore arguably clear that letter grades do not enhance learning for all students, it cannot be denied that they do genuinely motivate some learners—ourselves included, if truth be told. But even for those of us who are motivated by grades, we must wonder: What, exactly, compels this grade-oriented motivation? Do we value the learning that these grades represent to us, the evaluative judgments themselves (i.e., our teachers' approval and validation of our efforts and ourselves), or the progress made toward any number of different competitions in which good grades count as points scored? According to Richard Curwin (1976), students who receive good grades are pri-marily motivated to keep receiving them. "Good grades become more important to students who have accepted the notion that good grades mean good self-worth," he wrote (p. 141). Beyond voicing this alarm-ing relationship between grades and self-worth, Curwin extended his argument against the notion that grades are of educational value for even the most successful of students:

> It is highly unlikely that a good-grade getter will ever examine the process of his or her learning, for that can never be rewarded

by good grades. Neither will such students be motivated to behave creatively or uniquely. The fact is that grades can only be determined by accounting for the most insignificant aspects of learning. It is impossible to consider, in terms of letter grades, the values, feelings, creativity, intuition, judgment, higher levels of cognitive thinking, or any of the other things that truly influence the lives of students. (p. 141)

Some good-grade-getters, pressured to get more good grades, resort to cheating. Obviously the goal in this case is not to learn. Beyond whatever the effects may be on the heart, mind, and soul of the child who believes he must cheat to succeed, pressure to perform can take a crippling toll on the student who faces parental wrath or who self-inflicts undue emotional or physical punishment as a response to perceived failure.

According to Stephen Covey, a percentage system of grading promotes in many students such things as "mediocrity, pressure, paranoia, apathy, despair, greed, calculated behavior with no value investment, procrastination, anxiety, parental frustration, superiority, inferiority, cramming, and jealousy" (Covey as cited in Rogers, 1995). If the effects of grades on *good* students can be damaging, what of their effects on less capable ones? According to Rogers, grades are powerful destroyers of the motivation, behaviors, and performances that we want to see in kids. Further, he suggested a relationship between the practices of grading/ranking/sorting children and the reality that roughly one-fourth of all American students have either actively or passively given up on school by the end of the fifth grade and that half have done so by ninth grade (1995). While letter grades may be effective motivators for many students, for others, Kohn's warning (1993) appears to ring true: "Any time we are encouraged to focus on how well we are doing at something—as opposed to concentrating on the process of actually doing it—it is less likely that we will like the activity and keep doing it when given a choice" (p. 80).

LEARNER-CENTERED EVALUATION: REFRAMING THE PURPOSE OF GRADING

In the last section we discussed one aspect of the human cost associated with the use of grades and other forms of reward: intrinsic motivation is undermined. Associated with this intrinsic cost are the findings that with extrinsic motivators, learning becomes secondary to the grade, work is of lesser quality and creativity, and risk and growth are stifled in a "this for that" environment. Significant side effects in themselves, each of these recedes somewhat in the face of another blow to intrinsic motivation that is associated with the practice of using grades to sort and rank children: the disappearance of safety in many children's lives at school.

Abraham Maslow's name is immediately recognizable by most educators for his articulation of a "hierarchy of basic needs" (1943, Section III, ¶1). In describing five levels of human need (physical needs; safety needs; needs of love, affection, and belonging; needs for esteem; and needs for self-actualization), Maslow explained that a person will not feel a desire for the next level of need until the demands of the prior level have been satisfied. Significantly, awareness of higher concerns (e.g., aesthetic appreciation and spirituality) does not even exist until these five basic needs are met. Viewed through such a lens, it becomes apparent that a process of grading that is controlling, involving decisions that are all external to the child, can potentially threaten all but the most basic physical needs. A child whose work is consistently stamped deficient by her teachers (who in some cases are the most consistent adult presences in her life) is unlikely to feel safe, loved, or esteemed in the school setting. It is likely that her feelings of deficiency will extend into other settings as well and last beyond the school years.

The issue of safety in the classroom is also critical from a physiological perspective. In the presence of threat, the thinking, learning brain (the neocortex) cannot learn. At such times, it is controlled by the amygdala, an almond-shaped cluster on each side of the brain belonging to the limbic (oldest, "reptilian") brain. The amygdala acts as a scanner for trouble. If an incoming perception or situation presents itself as something that is hated, hurtful, or feared, the amygdala takes over and triggers a crisis message to all of the other parts of the brain. The older, reptilian brain is then in control until the threat is dealt with and the urgent "fight, freeze, or flee" impulse is resolved. During these times, the functioning of the neocortex is compromised. Simply put, it can't process and learn new academic content in the presence of danger. What about that child who gets D after D, F after F? If he is a student who can't read, for example, it's easily imaginable that he may be feeling unsafe in his classroom every day of the year. How much learning can he do if his amygdala is constantly busy running interference, trying to figure out how to keep him safe from the threat of being called upon to read out loud?

The processes of evaluating and reporting student growth offer us great opportunities to understand students' needs for self-determination, control, power, and the healthy development of identity. When those processes are inaccessible to students, there is little opportunity for the seeds of intrinsic desire to grow and little opportunity for those needs to be met. In her classic work on psychological theory and women's development, *In a Different Voice,* Carol Gilligan (1982) wrote two sentences that must critically inform educators' work with all of their students: "To have a voice is to be human. To have something to say is to be a person" (p. xvi). We think Gilligan was right, that being human is indeed about having a voice. It's about having a say in defining our own reality. When students are included in the process of making decisions about what matters in school—including decisions having to do with the curriculum, the learning activities, the assessment and evaluation procedures, and the establishment of standards—they are humanized.

Thirty years ago, before the existence of a report called *A Nation at Risk* or of legislation known as "No Child Left Behind," Arthur Combs (1976) wrote, "The real sickness of American education today is its irrelevance and dehumanization. We cannot afford to concentrate our evaluative devices upon less than the most important aspects of education" (p. 8). The challenge is clear for progressive and traditional educators alike. In concentrating our attention on evaluating and reporting student progress toward those "most important aspects of education," we must choose to value the needs and the voices of students.

Despite all of this, we are not advocating here for doing away with letter grades. We believe there are more important battles for progressive educators to fight (e.g., promoting the idea that while all educators must be accountable for giving all students access to rich and engaging learning environments and experiences, our nation must be held just as accountable for ensuring that all children have things like food, shelter, health care, excellent school facilities, and instructional resources). Furthermore, we believe that the processes of evaluating and reporting student growth can be made extraordinarily, educationally worthwhile—simply by involving students in those processes every step of the way.

FROM THEORY TO PRACTICE: STRATEGIES FOR EVALUATING AND REPORTING STUDENT GROWTH

Approach #1: Answer the crucial, fundamental question, "Progress toward what?" with your students.

Note that this strategy is linked to several suggestions from Chapter 3, "Observing and Assessing What Students Know and Can

Do." These include Approach #2, "Let students inside the assessment process"; Approach #3, "Involve students and parents in discussing and setting goals"; and Approach #4, "Be clear about where your instruction is headed before you begin teaching."

In a traditional classroom in which the content, purposes, and processes of evaluation are not explicitly known by students, letter grades can appear as mysteriously derived judgments determined by the teacher and given to students—not earned by them. Students may believe that grades represent anything from how smart they are to how well they do their homework to how much the teacher likes them to how influential their parents are. For learners to be able to attach genuine value and meaning to the processes of evaluating and reporting their growth, there can be no mysteries. If they are to care about the progress they are making, they have to be able to start out by knowing the details of just what it is that they're supposed to be making progress toward.

There's a simple test you can use to find out how well you're doing in the application of this approach. In each subject or course that you teach, ask your students to name, as specifically as they can, current knowledge goals ("What are you learning about this week in social studies?") and skills goals ("What are you learning to do in math this week?") The more specific their answers, the more empowered they will be to direct, assess, and evaluate their own learning. A student who knows that she's working to understand what place value has to do with solving three-column addition problems is more empowered as a learner than one who knows only that she is learning how to add, or even to solve three-column addition problems.

The question, "Progress toward what?" implies another question that students should also be able to answer: "Why does it matter?" If students are learning how to read latitude and longitude coordinates on a map but they haven't a clue as to why the concepts of latitude and longitude have any relevance in real life from their perspective, they are objects rather than subjects of your instruction.

Before you can empower your students by making sure they can name what they're learning and why it matters, you obviously must be able to answer those questions in specific detail yourself. As described in the previous two chapters, your answers to the "Progress toward what?" question will reflect (1) the skills your students have shown you that they are ready to learn and (2) the content-knowledge that your curriculum (your district- or state-level standards) defines as yours to teach.

Note that these curriculum documents typically define minimum standards. Depending upon what your students show you that they already know, nothing should keep you from extending your instruction to knowledge and skills beyond minimum requirements. Be warned, though, that the indefinite "should" in that sentence is an indicator of what can be a tricky situation. Sometimes educators in later grades are fiercely protective of what they see as their teaching turf. These tend to be content-oriented people who may not know how to build on what students already know and can do, so if you "take" their content, their approach to teaching is seriously compromised. It won't do any good to fight these folks, so work to understand their perspective. They, too, are doing the best they can, and they want to serve their students well. Where else can you look for ideas to extend your curriculum, other than through "their" novels or science projects or field trips? Other great books, community resources, and service-learning projects are always out there.

Finally, in keeping with the ideal of establishing a safe, inclusive community in your classroom, students should be able to explain that skills-based goals in their classroom tend to be defined differently for each learner, while content-knowledge goals are generally more applicable to the community as a whole.

Approach #2: Nurture a growth orientation rather than a perfection orientation to the processes of assessment and evaluation.

Be explicit in your own mind, with your students, and with their parents that your concern is with your students' progress, not their perfection. This is such a crucial concept, because the mind-set that you bring to evaluation determines how you will see your kids in the process. Our expectations are extraordinarily powerful in defining what we are capable of seeing.

A teacher who approaches evaluation from a perfection orientation is focused on what her students are supposed to know, rather than on what they do know. Her content-centered rather than child-centered approach to assessment and evaluation means that the achievement of content-knowledge perfection is the only target she knows how to define. In this evaluative context, the 100% mark is a more important goal than that of individual growth.

A teacher who approaches evaluation from a growth orientation uses assessment and observation strategies (see Chapter 3) to continuously document what his students know and can do; he uses periodic evaluations to reflect his judgments (and those of his students, when possible) about their achievements over time, using clearly defined performance standards to contextualize those judgments and give them meaning. This is not to say that letter grades for this teacher are all about sending feel-good messages to students; his grading practices also reflect the accuracy of students' understandings as demonstrated in the correctness of their work. (Ideas about how to address both effort and accuracy while evaluating students are offered below, in Approach #3.) A growth-oriented teacher simply recognizes the fact that success breeds success. By focusing and building on what his students *can* do, he can help them *want* to accomplish more. While a perfection orientation may encourage some students to reach for the A+, it encourages many more—the ones who aren't even close to being in arm's reach of academic perfection—to figure out in precise detail how little they can do and still earn a C or to choose "failure" intentionally. These students know they will never win the competition of the perfection game, so their concern is with choosing to "pass" or not rather than with the processes of thinking, learning, and growing.

Being clear with yourself, your students, and their parents about the value of growth will help to focus your collective attention on the fundamental importance of what you're doing together and why it matters to begin with. Being explicit about the idea that achievement has more to do with growth than perfection can also help students to relax into the hard work of learning, knowing that in your classroom, at least, school is about challenges, not competitions.

Approach #3: If you have to give letter grades, as most teachers in the intermediate grades and above do, involve students in establishing criteria for them.

One way to do this is to follow the process described in Chapter 3 (Approach #4) and create a grading rubric with your students for each content area or course that you teach. Start the conversation with your students by provoking their interest in the topic. Invite kids to talk, even to argue, their way toward what they believe in response to questions like these:

- What grade do you think a student has earned in math if he does all of his homework all of the time, always pays attention and tries as hard as he can in class, but gets just as many wrong answers as right ones on his homework and tests?

- What grade would you give a student who never does her math homework, goofs around and bothers other people in class, but always gets 100% on her tests?
- What does an A mean? How about an F? What does it mean to be "average" in (math)?

In our experience, students in intermediate grades and above have clear ideas about what it takes to earn an A or an F and every designation in between. They tend to believe (as we do) that grades should reflect both effort and accuracy. Giving students the opportunity to define what must be true for them to earn an A in the different subjects (or a B, C, D, or F) honors their knowledge and gives them a powerful, meaningful voice in the evaluation process.

About halfway through the first quarter of the school year, Kaia used the questions above to launch a discussion about grading with her fifth graders. During the course of the fifth week of school, the class then created one grading rubric a day (for math, reading, writing, science, and social studies), and they used those rubrics at the end of the week to write about how they were doing so far that quarter. (Writing prompt: "If you had to give yourself a grade right now in each area, what would it be? Why? Defend your opinions with evidence.")

You'll recognize the procedure they followed in creating those rubrics from Chapter 3. In writing the first rubric for grading in math, the class began by brainstorming everything they could think of that would be true for a student who earns an A. Then they categorized those ideas, labeled the categories with trait names, and brainstormed descriptors for each "A-level" trait. Then they did the same for the opposite end of the spectrum, defining what would be true for a student who earns an F (using the same traits that they already identified but defining them this time in failing terms). Finally, they drew from both the A and F trait descriptions and wrote a description of each trait for the grade of C. They talked about how they would go about deciding if they had earned a B or D using that rubric (operating between the A and C or the C and F descriptions), and they talked about the importance of evidence in using those rubrics to evaluate their performances. To illustrate, Figure 5.1 shows the math rubric the class created (with a fair amount of instructional input and facilitation).

Finally, Kaia asked what should happen if she and a student disagreed at the end of the quarter about what grade to write on the student's report card. They came up with the following procedure together: (1) Students would look through their working portfolios and their grade graphs (more on this in Approach #4, below) in each

Figure 5.1   Math Grading Rubric

Math Grading Rubric			Student: _____ Date: _____
Directions: Circle the dots by the descriptions that describe you. (If you fall in between A and C or between C and F, draw a dot on the line in the middle and circle it.) Then look at the pattern of all of the circles and decide if you think you have earned an A, B, C, D, or F in math this quarter. Be prepared to back your judgment with evidence!			
	Students who earn an "A":	*Students who earn a "C":*	*Students who earn an "F":*
Work Ethic (Effort)	• Try hard to do their very best on every class activity and assignment • Are willing to take risks and explain their thinking about math problems • Always complete all homework assignments thoroughly • Always show their work; papers are clear and well organized	• Usually do just enough to get by on class activities and homework • Can explain their thinking about math problems but would rather play it safe and let others do it • Complete about three-fourths of all homework assignments • Papers are often on the sloppy side and disorganized; it's often hard to tell where answers came from	• Don't put much effort into their work • Don't try to explain their thinking; won't take chances • Complete half or less than half of all homework assignments • Don't show where answers came from; work is disorganized
Knowledge and Skills (Accuracy)	• Can interpret math problems on their own, and can explain which procedures to use in solving them • Can explain how they solved the problem and if the answer makes sense • Homework average from grade graphs is between 90%–100% (____%) • Test score average is between 90%–100% (____%)	• Can solve math problems correctly when someone else explains them and shows which procedures are needed • Can explain how they got an answer but may not be able to tell if it makes sense • Homework average from grade graphs is 70%–79% (____%) • Test score average is 70%–79% (____)	• Don't know how to set up or solve math problems on their own • Can't explain where answers came from or if they make sense • Homework average from grade graphs is 59% or below (____%) • Test score average is 59% or below (____%)

subject, looking especially at assessment feedback; (2) students would write a paragraph about what grade they should get for each area (including "+" and "−" grades, that is, A+ or A−, etc.), defending their judgments with whatever evidence they could find; (3) Kaia would review students' self-evaluations and schedule a conference with any student with whom she disagreed. She and the student would argue their cases with each other and try to find an acceptable compromise. If an acceptable compromise couldn't be reached, students would agree to abide by their teacher's final judgment as long as they could appeal it to the principal.

Not once during the year was a decision appealed, seldom were individual conferences required, and grading disagreements were just as often because students were too hard on themselves as too easy (a phenomenon to which female students seem particularly prone). Students' participation in defining standards and then using those standards to assess their own performances made the grading process more meaningful to them. In thinking about the evaluation process, they were able to focus more on their performances as learners than on their grades—a phenomenon that is also typically evident when adult learners are asked to reflect upon a similar experience in Kaia's methods courses: "The grading procedure made me think of my own performance, not working for someone else," wrote one, while another observed, "I think that the untraditional approach to grading, once I got used to the idea, was much more effective in challenging me as a student and authentically assessing my growth." Involving students in evaluating their performances in our classrooms can powerfully impact their desire to learn, evidenced by the adult learner who wrote, "Rating myself made me think about how much effort I really put in assignments and made me want to put in more effort."

Approach #4: Implement student-led parent conferences.

Parents often associate feeling excluded, devalued, rushed, and powerless in the context of the traditional parent-teacher conference. Educators are also often frustrated with the experience, particularly middle and high school teachers, who are expected to communicate meaningfully with 100–150 families in three to five days' time. Teachers are often urged to make more time available for families who require evening or weekend conference times, but compensation for that time away from their own families is seldom forthcoming. For many reasons, the formal sharing of information about students' progress through traditional parent-teacher conferences is a stressful, frustrating experience for many parents and teachers. Furthermore, these traditional conferences are more likely than not to exclude the very person whose growth as a learner is being discussed. Finding ways for students to participate meaningfully in these conferences is a beginning step toward making the reporting of student progress meaningful for everyone involved.

In *Changing the View: Student-Led Parent Conferences*, Terri Austin (1994) described the process she follows throughout the year to allow her students a lead role in evaluating their own academic progress and reporting it to their parents. Her logic was that when students are excluded from the parent-teacher conference, the most important voice that can genuinely speak to the question of what was learned that quarter has been silenced. She advocated not only for students to participate in conferences but to lead them. We recommend her highly readable book for a detailed description of how to structure the process. Also, even if you decide not to pursue full-blown student-led conferences, we urge you at least to include students in student-teacher-parent conferences and find meaningful ways for them to participate as subjects in (rather than objects of) the conversation.

Student-led parent conferences provide an effective way for teachers to address the problem of parents' feeling excluded, devalued, rushed, and powerless, for the simple reason that they can be scheduled so as to allow parents more time for the conversation. They can have the time they need to see evidence of what their child has learned, to ask questions, to participate in the process of evaluating whether that quarter's goals were met, and to help identify appropriate goals for the upcoming quarter. Kaia's approach was to schedule hour-long conferences with each family and to schedule three families' conferences at the same time. For each family, she would lead a 20-minute conversation, sharing her observations about the student's progress and reviewing the report card; this left the student 40 minutes to lead a discussion with the parents about the contents of their conference portfolio.

Three conference areas were set up in the room, along with a table for refreshments. When families arrived, the students were responsible for escorting their parents (and grandparents, aunts, uncles, and siblings, who frequently came along) to a conference area, seating them, and serving them juice and cookies. Then the student would go to the conference portfolio file box, retrieve his or her portfolio, and begin working through the conference agenda and accompanying samples of student work inside the portfolio. (During the week prior to conferences, students were guided through the processes of brainstorming possible agenda items for conferences, finalizing their conference agenda, selecting representative samples of work, and writing reflections for each sample, indicating why it was important in the context of their learning goals.) The following is a sample "Student-Parent-Teacher Conference Agenda" that Kaia created for fall conferences, after her fifth graders brainstormed ideas about what they could include in their conference portfolios to represent that quarter's work in each subject area and in interdisciplinary study.

STUDENT-PARENT-TEACHER CONFERENCE AGENDA

Part I: Student-Led Portion of the Student-Parent-Teacher Conference (40 minutes)

1. Writer's Workshop/Author's Chair

- Read at least two pieces from Writer's Workshop aloud to your parents.
- Share your written reflections on those pieces with your parents. Read your reflections aloud; then ask your parents, "How do my reflections help you to understand what I've been learning about in Writer's Workshop?" Get them to explain their answer.
- Show your parents a piece that you've written that you're not entirely happy with. Explain why.
- Choose one of your pieces to assess with your parent's help, using the six-trait rubrics. Work together to decide what level you're at in the three areas we've been working on: Voice, Ideas, and Conventions.
- Brainstorm with your parents new ideas that you could write about and add those to your topic list in your Writer's Workshop Binder.

2. Math

- Share your written reflection about what you've been learning in math. Read this aloud to your parents.
- Show your Math Review Packet. Show which problems are easy for you to do on your own and which ones you're not quite able to do by yourself yet. Let them choose two or three problems for

you to demonstrate. Invite them to coach you through a couple of the difficult problems if they want.

- Play a math game with your parents. You may choose Factor Captor or Multiplication Wrestling or challenge them to a round or two of Mad Minute.

3. Reading

- Show your parents the book that you're reading in your Literature Circle. Explain what is happening in the book so far. Show them your Story Web for your book.
- Read at least two or three pages aloud to them.
- Share your written reflections about Socratic Discussion. Explain what we do during that time and what you're learning from it.

4. Social Studies

- Share one of the readings we've studied together during Social Studies/Socratic Discussion time. Talk about what the piece means to you or what you learned from it.
- Show your parents your U.S. History Time Line. See if they can add to it by filling in two or three events and dates that we haven't studied yet.

5. Science

- Describe the five steps of the scientific process to your parents. Explain why it is important to control your variables. Give an example.
- Share your Science Fair question. Ask your parents to brainstorm with you some ideas for how to state your hypothesis and to design your experiment.

6. Other

- Share your written reflections about how our class is running and about how you're doing in the area of taking responsibility for your own behavior and learning. Show them your Behavioral Self-Assessment from last week.
- Show your parents your grade graphs from last quarter and your new ones for this quarter. Explain what the graphs tell about who you are as a student, from your point of view. Then ask them,

"What do these graphs tell you?" Note: Grade graphing, the creation of a visual picture of students' recorded grades in each subject area, is a strategy that Austin (1994) described in *Changing the View*. Students create a bar graph for each subject; the teacher meets periodically with each student and reads their recorded grades, which students transcribe and plot on their various subject-area graphs. At the end of the grading period, for each subject-area graph, the student averages his or her assignment grades three times, then has a partner average them until both agree on the final average score in each subject. The power of the graph is in the picture it creates. Kaia had students take grade graphs and working portfolios home regularly during the course of a quarter for parents' review and signature.

7. Write With Your Parents

- What goals will you set for this quarter? What will you accomplish as
  o a writer;
  o a reader;
  o a mathematician;
  o a scientist;
  o a student of social studies; and
  o an artist?

**Part II: Teacher-Led Portion of the
Student-Parent-Teacher Conference (20 minutes)**

1. My Observations as Your Teacher: What do I see as your strengths as a student? What areas seem to be hard for you? What do we need to focus on (teacher, student, and parent) to support further growth?

2. Report Card

3. Questions/Conversation

4. Teacher Evaluation/Feedback Form (completed by parents)

An inclusive approach to reporting student progress reflects the belief that students are the primary owners of their learning and that, with support, they can tell what they have learned more accurately than anyone else. Finally, it is a way of making student progress visible to students themselves, to their parents, and to their teachers. This is the stuff that intrinsic motivation is made of.

SUMMARY

The processes of evaluating and reporting student growth can be made extraordinarily, educationally worthwhile. We recommended the following strategies for involving students in those processes at every step of the way:

- *Answer the crucial, fundamental question, "Progress toward what?" with your students.* Before you can empower your students by making sure they can name what they're learning and why it matters, you obviously must be able to answer those questions in specific detail yourself.
- *Nurture a growth orientation rather than a perfection orientation to the processes of assessment and evaluation.* Be explicit in your own mind, with your students, and with their parents that your concern is with your students' progress, not their perfection.
- *If you are required to give letter grades, involve students in establishing criteria for them.* Giving students the opportunity to define the requirements for earning an A (or a B, C, D, or F) honors their knowledge and gives them a powerful, meaningful voice in evaluation process.
- *Implement student-led parent conferences.* Finding ways for students to participate meaningfully in conferences makes the reporting of student progress valuable for everyone involved and allows students to participate as subjects in (rather than objects of) the conversation.

6

Facilitating Community Development With Parents

Celina laughs at herself now, when she thinks about how much she didn't know as a parent when her kids were in elementary school. She has learned a lot since then and has become a powerful advocate for other families in her mostly Hispanic community. Back then, though, she was like many parents: fearful and unsure, an outsider in her children's school.

She describes the first individualized educational program meeting she ever attended, paralyzed with fear about what it might mean that so many educators needed to meet with her to discuss her daughter. "I've got to watch my p's and q's," she thought to herself throughout that terrifying meeting. "I can't show I'm mad, because what if they take my daughter away from me?"

"That's how naïve I was," she laughs, and then adds quietly, "or intimidated. Or not knowing. Not knowing."

Today, Celina uses what she has learned over the years to help other parents in her community to understand how the system works. She talks with parents who want to know, "Why does the teacher pay attention to that parent and not me? I have the same questions!"

"These are true stories!" she exclaims. "They are stories that I can tell you from our neighborhood. It was Open House at the school, and the people from our neighborhood felt ignored. What was the difference? Because the other parents asked the right questions? Used the right words? And all you said was, well, you just wanted to know how your daughter was doing."

> *Celina's friend, Elena, agrees that not all parents are helped to feel like valued members of their school community. "If this parent who is a college graduate comes into school and says, 'I'm Mrs. So-and-So, and my husband is an attorney,' it says something. There is a different way of dealing with that parent. Then I come in. 'My name is Elena Torres, I only graduated from high school, and my husband is in construction.' Well, then there is a different way of dealing with me because of who I am, because of our education. So they assume. They assume that we aren't as smart."*

Our ability to listen with sincerity and respect and our willingness to communicate honestly are two things that largely determine the quality of our relationships in the classroom—not only with our students, but with their parents as well. Parents are members of the classroom community, too, and they must be intentionally included in the processes of developing it. Essential questions that each of us must be able to answer in the emphatic affirmative—before we approach parents with the goal of developing a genuine sense of community with them—are these: Do I have a sincere desire to create space for parents' voices? Do I value their observations regarding their child, their ideas about education, and their perceptions of their child's experience in my classroom? Am I willing, in turn, to caringly, honestly share with them my questions, concerns, and observations about their child's academic and social development?

The ideal of *educere* requires respectful listening and straightforward communication, but these tend to be more the exception than the rule when it comes to characterizing typical teacher-parent interactions. Many new teachers (and some experienced ones as well) approach the prospect of talking with their students' parents with feelings of apprehension, self-doubt, and fear. These feelings can cause some teachers to talk to parents superficially, either by offering bland pleasantries and generalizations or by talking through their grade books, relying on the dispassionate authority of numbers rather than on their ability to facilitate genuine conversation focused on the mutual exchange of informed observations. The sad irony is that many parents approach teachers with the same feelings of insecurity, anxiety, and fear—a reality that is particularly likely for parents who are poor, for those who identify in some way outside of the dominant culture that is typically reinforced in schools, and for parents whose own experiences in school were negative.

The basic challenge for the progressive educator seeking to develop community with parents is to escape the prevailing pattern of mutual apprehension that defines too many parent-teacher interactions and to pursue instead a new dynamic in which mutual authority is consciously, purposefully honored. Parker Palmer (1993), author and founder of the Courage to Teach program, offered a useful starting point for teachers interested in pursuing this project: for mutual authority to be honored, we must be as willing to listen as we are willing to speak. "It takes humility for a teacher to create and sustain silence, a silence in which we withhold the instant answer so the question can really be heard," wrote Palmer. "The teacher who lacks humility will be unable to create a space for any voice except his or her own" (p. 109).

In other words, the progressive teacher must be deeply, intentionally committed to the essential equality of authority among all parties in the parent-teacher relationship. On one hand, teachers must be comfortable with their own authority when communicating with parents, and that authority must be grounded in the attributes of confidence and humility. On the other, they must be willing and able not only to honor but also to encourage, when necessary, the same kind of authority in parents. A parent and a teacher know different things about the same child; when both perspectives are valued, the child can be more fully known and supported. (Besides, with challenging kids, parents are often flailing at home as desperately as we are at school. At least by joining the struggle together as equals, a coherent plan can be formed for helping these students.)

For the teacher who is developing that balance of confidence and humility, who is learning to find her authoritative (not authoritarian) stride when communicating with parents, it is useful to reflect on the meaning of these two attributes in this new context. When communicating with parents, confidence comes first and foremost from knowing the child. What parents typically want, more than anything, is to know that you are truly paying attention to what is—hands down, for the vast majority—the most excruciatingly precious part of their lives. They want to see and hear evidence that you know their child. They want proof that you understand what he is going through at school, that you like and believe in him, and that, in knowing him, you know how to challenge him as well. Demonstrating your knowledge about this child requires your considerable skill as a scientist. If you are not a keen observer of your students and a careful, habitual documenter of those observations, your communications with parents are likely to be superficial and predictable. One of the fathers interviewed by Sarah Lawrence-Lightfoot (2003) described these kinds of empty interactions as "hiding behind the ritual":

As he sits in the first parent meeting of the year for his son, who is in third grade, Andrew Green tries to push the teacher past her ritualistic reporting, past the usual platitudes that tend to define the first cautious encounters. In the opening minutes of the conference, he hears what he already knows and what he expects, and he grows impatient. The teacher reports that Alex is in tutoring, that he is in the third reading group, et cetera. "All they are doing," says Andrew, "is hiding behind the ritual, reciting facts." He holds up his hands above his head. "They are starting way up here, saying all the stuff that is already observable to me. . . . I am trying to get them to be more descriptive of what's going on, to move beyond the abstractions and the bland, empty platitudes. . . . In other words, I want to know what the teacher has observed that leads her to make these judgments . . . and I want to know how these judgments stack up relative to what set of expectations." (p. 76)

These are clearly the words of a frustrated parent. Unfortunately, while this father is able to articulate what he needs from his son's teachers, he doesn't know how to ask for it in the moment in a way that his son's teacher can hear; he doesn't know how to help this teacher to provide the specifics that would, for him, bring the conversation from the realm of empty ritual to a meaningful sharing of observations and ideas. Instead, as one experienced teacher we know who read his words put it, his frustrations come across as vaguely threatening: "His hands in the air and his impatience have shut down the lines of communication for me," she said. "If I were his son's teacher, I'd just want to get out of there, now." With frustration, anxiety, and defensiveness more the norm than the exception in defining typical parent-teacher interactions, hiding behind the ritual is a logical, safe, and thoroughly unproductive option for parents and teachers alike.

Many teachers and parents can't help but bring defensiveness to their conversations with one another, because they've been set up for it. When the educational emphasis throughout a society is overwhelmingly focused on what children are supposed to know, rather than on what they do know and therefore on what is evident as next for them to learn, parent-teacher conversations are destined to be approached from a deficit-oriented perspective that emphasizes conformity to grade-level expectations more than individual children's interests, abilities, and developmental needs. In a system bent on standardizing children's knowledge and skills, a student's academic progress is synonymous with how well she is able to conform, to blend in with those expectations. With conformity rather than the ideals of *educere* established as the primary value in our schools, parent-teacher interactions have an entirely logical, predictable tendency toward conflict.

The sources of the parents' side of that conflict lie in their concern about how their child compares with the other students in the class, their fear that their child isn't okay or progressing sufficiently in the right way, and their feelings of anxiousness and powerlessness in the realization that their authority may or may not be genuinely valued in their particular school context. For teachers who have been encouraged to believe that students' academic achievements must be measured against standard grade-level expectations, conflicted feelings when communicating with parents can come from worries of inadequacy. In schools that operate on the controlling principles of behaviorism, teachers are socially defined as knowers, not seekers. They are presumed to be directors, not partners in the parent-teacher relationship. Hiding behind the ritual of grade books and bland observations is a reasonable but ineffectual response to an unreasonable and ineffectual conception of what it means to be a teacher.

The good news is that, in this educational arena as much as any other, the paradigm of behaviorism can be consciously rejected in favor of a learner-centered ideology. When parents and teachers can share their genuine questions and focused observations with each other, a learner-centered approach to communication can release both parties from the feelings of inadequacy, anxiety, frustration, and fear that are so common in the traditional, control-oriented script that parents and teachers alike tend to follow.

This approach also honors the needs and rights of parents to know important, specific details about their child's everyday experiences in your classroom. This is precisely what Alex's father was able to articulate in the quote above, if not to his son's teacher. He named exactly what he would need from you, if you were that teacher, to know that his son was in skilled and knowledgeable hands. He said that he would want you to be descriptive, sharing specific observations about his son's activities in your classroom that inform your judgments about the boy's academic progress, and he would want to know what criteria you used as the basis for those judgments. These are specific, feasible, and necessary things for teachers to be able to discuss with parents.

For beginning teachers, it can be helpful to have a general format in mind when speaking with parents about their child's academic performance. A good conferencing plan is one that will show parents that you know their child and, therefore, one that will allow you to approach them with confidence. The following five-part conference format is one that Monica uses to structure her conversations with parents: (1) This is what I know about your child's development (in each subject), (2) this is how I know it (using specific developmental rubrics and other assessment instruments available and providing copies of these documents for parents), (3) this is what I see as next for him to work toward (again using developmental rubrics as guides), (4) these are some of the ways we'll be working on those goals in class, and (5) here are some strategies you could use at home.

Having the ability to be descriptive about what you know about your students—that is, moving beyond abstractions to share real insights—requires the cultivation of observation as a purposeful habit. By making a point of seeing and recording the details of Alex's academic and social development in your classroom, you will have created a solid foundation upon which meaningful conversation with his father can occur. You will then be able to offer him the detailed information he needs in order to know that you're paying attention, that you know his son, and that the two of you share the same interest of doing right by the boy. Specific strategies for observing and assessing what students know and can do were described in Chapter 3, and strategies for facilitating effective student-parent-teacher conferences were offered in Chapter 5. The relevant point for this chapter on facilitating community development with parents is simply that detailed, two-way communication is both a prerequisite for and a means of accomplishing that goal. Through knowing our students and exchanging with parents our informed views, successes, and failures, true and trusting partnerships can be created. Doing this requires (and builds) confidence and humility, in equal measure.

> During a parent-teacher conference early in her teaching career, Jeanine confessed to Molly that she wasn't feeling successful in teaching the woman's brilliant sixth-grade son. By explaining why she was feeling inadequate and by sharing her observations about this student's apparent boredom and disengagement in her class, she opened the way for a genuine and productive parent-teacher conversation about the boy as a person and as a learner. Several years later, when Molly came to work in the school at which Jeanine was now principal, she reminded Jeanine of the conference many years before that had featured her feelings of failure as Ian's teacher. And then Molly said, "That's when I knew I could trust you."

Confidence also comes from your strength of purpose and vision, from being able to articulate your goals for the children in your care; it comes from knowing your content well and being able to discuss why it is relevant in the particular circumstances of your students' lives. Having confidence in communicating with parents requires the courage to share your thoughts honestly, the courage to be vulnerable enough to welcome critical questions and concerns, and the courage to stand firm by your best judgment and professional values when faced with a parent who is unwilling to honor your authority and/or your right to be treated with dignity. (More on this particular challenge in Approach #4 below.)

Humility comes from understanding that your knowledge of your students may be different from their parents' knowledge but not superior to it, and it comes from the absolute certainty that you, your students, and their parents will make mistakes during the year. If you have the confidence to talk at the beginning of the year with parents and students about the value of mistakes in the learning process (see Approach #3 below)—whether they are made by students, the parent, or you—you will have taken one step toward creating an open, honest environment for home-school communication that has the potential for leading to an actual partnership.

When thinking about the presence of humility as an essential attribute in teacher-parent relationships, it is important to hold a caution in mind: excessive deference does not serve the goal of community development. Too much humility on either part is as potentially damaging to home-school partnerships as an excess of confidence. Genuine authority is found in the artful and often-difficult balancing of the two.

Developing community with parents requires your faith in the fact that the vast majority are highly reasonable and supportive people who want to help you, because they know that you are in a very powerful position to help (or to harm) their children. This is not to say that "difficult" parents aren't out there. They are, but even the majority of these can be reasonable when they are helped to feel safe, valued, capable, and powerful. Parents do not tend to expect perfection in you any more than they do in themselves; they value your humanity and your ability to responsibly model what it means to be human—to be both great and fallible—with their children. They are typically quick to forgive and quick to support you when they are confident in your good intentions for their child; when they can trust that you have vision, knowledge, and skills; and when they are certain of your respect for their authority and perspectives.

FROM THEORY TO PRACTICE: STRATEGIES FOR FACILITATING COMMUNITY DEVELOPMENT WITH PARENTS

Approach #1: Do all that you can think of, and then think and do more, to make your parents feel comfortable with you and in their child's classroom.

It is the rare parent who can walk into a school or a classroom and feel completely at ease, confident of his or her power in this environment, which probably feels as natural and comfortable to you (or soon will) as your own home. When parents come to you, a good number of them will not arrive already trusting that your classroom will be a good place for their children to be or where they themselves will feel welcome. Whether this initial insecurity is because of their own history in school; because of social, cultural, and economic realities that make school success more likely for some children than for others; or simply because there is so much at stake, the reality for most parents is that school is not a place where they enjoy a strong sense of authority in their children's lives. A mother we know who is Navajo, and who is also an activist working to help Native American students and families fight for their rights in schools and in the broader society, explained:

> I keep stressing in my community, to Native parents, that they need to be aware of their rights. That they have the power to tell the principal that their children have that right, to have an education. And you know, it's kind of hard to make them think that, because of how they grew up. They were taught that the teachers and administrators are way up here, and they're down here. So to convince them that they have that power, you know, how do you do that?

While we believe it is true that vocal parents can wield a great deal of power in a school or district, these people represent a small fraction of the population. The great majority of parents, particularly those who are poor or otherwise living realities that exist outside the mainstream of dominant culture, feel anything but powerful when they are on your turf. Your challenge is to help them to understand that your classroom is their turf, too.

A necessary first step in this is simply to be a good host. Having a parent in your room at the start of the year is similar to having a likable new neighbor over to your home. Think of the things you would do to make this neighbor feel welcome, to help her to know that you are sincerely glad she has come. You would greet her at the door; you would call her by name; you would invite her to sit. (It should go without saying that the chair you provide for a parent should be of the same quality and size as the one you use. Remarkably, though, one mother told us that one of her son's elementary teachers always provided her with a tiny child's chair while she sat tall in her cushioned teacher's chair! Teachers and parents, hosts and guests, should be seated as equals. As soon as you take the better chair or have a seat behind your desk, you will have clearly established the ground rule of inequality in your teacher-parent relationships.) After inviting your neighbor inside, as a good host, you would ask your guest appropriate questions to encourage her to talk, and you would focus on being a good listener. You would ask her to make herself at home; you'd probably encourage her to stop by again any time.

Imagine how unwelcome and unimportant this woman would feel if you invited her over, sat her down on a footstool while you took the recliner, and then did most of the talking. Imagine how eager she would be to leave your horrible home if you ended the visit by telling her to make sure to call ahead next time to see if you want her to come over. When parents are not helped to feel like welcome and valued members of the community who are free to drop by their child's classroom at any time, they know they are outsiders, powerless in their lack of belonging.

Having parents in your classroom at the beginning of the year, while you are just starting to get to know each other, is really no different than having that guest in your home. (If the parent is obnoxious and demanding, a special challenge exists, which Approach #4 addresses below.) The reality is that since the parent-teacher dynamic happens mostly in your territory, the responsibility for how the relationship develops is largely yours. As the year progresses, that responsibility can be more evenly shared; but in the beginning, most parents unfortunately know from experience that it's your court, your ball, your game. Parents with a lot of cultural capital (i.e., those whose cultural values and practices are aligned with the dominant-culture norms that tend to be reinforced in schools) will at least know how the game is played. These parents may have a chance to feel a measure of power and influence in their children's education, with or without you. But for parents without the "right" cultural capital, for those who may lack social or economic power, and for many of those who have children with special needs, the game is an unfamiliar one that must be learned while they are playing it on a foreign field. It's your job to help them to relax and have fun with it, even to enjoy the process of participating in their child's education.

Another part of helping parents to feel comfortable is to let them know who you are. Why did you decide to be a teacher? What are some of the things that you care deeply about? What do you most enjoy in life? One way to broach this sharing of personal information, since many parents will not feel it is their place to ask for it, might be to say something like, "So, we've spent a lot of time talking about Ashley; what is it about me or my teaching that you might like to know?" A partnership of equals presumes two-way communication, two-way knowledge. It may be that you share information about yourself only once, at the beginning of the year, since the purpose of your parent-teacher partnership is to focus on the needs of the child you have in common. But if parents are ever to feel comfortable enough to ask you important questions or to engage in genuine, substantive conversation with you, they need to know and trust you. They deserve to know the person they are entrusting with the care and education of their children. Maria, a parent activist and student/family advocate in her community, put it this way:

> I noticed that teachers saw our children through the grade book, and that really bothered me. And then, they get to business right away. A lot of parents want to get to know the teacher! How are you? Where do you live? Just, how do you say, *charla*, to have conversation that makes people feel comfortable.

All of this is not to say that your goal must be to develop friendships with your students' parents. It is your responsibility, rather, to serve your *students'* needs by facilitating the development of relationships with their parents that are grounded in respect, equality, and in the recognition of mutual authority. You will set the tone. Parents will learn to trust that you can provide a good learning environment for their child when they can feel for themselves that your classroom is a good place to be.

Approach #2: Give parents great reasons to be in your classroom by continually giving their children opportunities to shine there.

For many parents, your good hosting habits and your open, respectful communication style will be enough to make them feel welcome and comfortable in your classroom. For many others, though, school is a place that is simply too intimidating, too uncomfortable, too foreign to make being there feel good. Boyoyo, a master teacher whose middle school science classes are conducted in his first language of Spanish, explained this reality:

> I'm telling you, coming from another country, we are kind of afraid because of language. And there are a lot of things. There is a lot of worry. Parents feel afraid because they do not know what's going on. I think this is why we don't get involved in all of what's going on. I think there are a lot of parents that, because of work, because of the level of education, sometimes they don't have the time, sometimes they feel afraid to go and express themselves. I can tell you, I was going to meetings with my daughters, and I was just trying to understand what is going on. So how can I express myself, if I don't understand what's going on?

Whatever the reasons for many parents' feelings of discomfort in school, it is a virtual certainty that you will be working with students whose parents will need to be helped to become involved in their children's experience in your classroom. While the reasons for a seeming lack of involvement may not be obviously apparent to you, what is clear beyond question is the need for you to go out of your way in helping parents to become engaged in their children's school lives. A lack of parental involvement is said to be the biggest problem facing public schools (Michigan Department of Education, 2002), an unfortunate reality given the substantial benefits that academically engaged parents offer their children. These students have "higher grades, test scores, and graduation rates; better school attendance; increased motivation and better self-esteem; lower rates of suspension; decreased use of drugs and alcohol; and fewer instances of violent behavior. Family participation in education is twice as predictive of students' academic success as family socioeconomic status" (Michigan Department of Education, Impact section, ¶3).

The question, then, is not whether to encourage parents' involvement in their child's experience with school, but how. The answer lies in the same body of research described in Chapter 1 on facilitating community development in the classroom. Just like children, we adults need to feel safe, valued, powerful, and capable, and we must feel enjoyment, to be intrinsically motivated to engage in any particular behavior. Seemingly uninvolved parents may not show up in your classroom because any number of these prerequisites for intrinsic motivation and self-esteem is missing. In Approach #1, we offered ideas about how to facilitate parents' likelihood of feeling valued and powerful (i.e., having authority), and strategies for helping them to feel capable as supporters of their children's learning goals were discussed in Chapters 3 and 5. What remains for this discussion is how to provide opportunities for parents to experience feelings of safety so they can enjoy opportunities to participate in their child's life at school.

Putting energy into communicating with parents may seem an impossible task given the inhuman demands on educators' "off" time, particularly for new teachers. But this is another instance in which time spent initially is guaranteed to save a tremendous amount of time and energy in the long run. Communicating regularly with parents will help them to trust you, to feel safe in knowing that their child is in good hands. Making a point of documenting the good things you see in a child's academic and social development will give you reasons to communicate with parents on a regular basis—*before* Carmen decides to toss a rock through a window during recess or to convince her gullible classmate that it would be a good idea for him to wash his hands in the girls' bathroom. These kinds of problems *will* be coming up in your class; after all, it's every kid's job to learn where the boundaries are and find out what they can get away with. For you and Carmen's parents to be able to encourage her to take responsibility for her actions when she behaves nastily, it will help if they already know that you can see what a great kid she is. Sometimes, it's true, you will have to be willing to take that on faith and to operate on the presumption that she has the potential for greatness. Searching for authentic, good news to share in this case is especially important, since you'll probably be working to overcome years of the bad news stories these parents are used to hearing.

The bottom line is this: you must spend time right away, especially, but also throughout the year, intentionally looking for specific details that tell you what is good and promising in each one of your students. Send e-mails, write notes, or make telephone calls just to say that you were impressed with Carmen's insightful comment during a recent class discussion (and describe the particulars) or that you noticed her going out of her way to stick up for her gullible classmate at recess. Our bias is that you should not make a handy, institutional-looking form for this purpose; keep it more personal, more spontaneous, and more genuine than that, or even design clever stationery specifically for your good-news notes. For example, a student-teacher we know created good-news stationery in the form of a 3×6 inch electric guitar. On the front of it, she wrote, "Dylan rocks!" and on the back, she recorded the details that led her to think so.

Sending physical notes for this purpose rather than always relying on telephone calls or e-mail serves another purpose. These notes tend to live long, proud lives on refrigerator doors—giving younger kids (and we suspect many older ones, too) cause for often much-needed academic pride and encouragement. Do not attach rewards to these positive behaviors you're noting. You're not trying to buy more good behavior from students through these positive connections with parents; you're simply recognizing and celebrating the fact that kids are doing what they should, and you're building stronger relationships with both students and parents in the process.

When you do need to contact Carmen's parents because she threw a rock at a window or did some hurtful thing to a classmate, do it immediately. Communicate your concern, even your frustration, but never angrily; talk about how you handled it and why. If further consequences are necessary, invite the parent to discuss possibilities with you and the student. (Sometimes this may not be possible, if the incident was serious enough to trigger automatic school/district-level policies.) Finally, share your vision of how this incident informs the larger picture of the goals that you, Carmen, and her parents have for her academic and social growth. In other words, how can this bad choice on her part be productively used to help her become more conscious of the importance of those goals and to involve her in planning for her improvement in those areas?

Another way to help parents experience feelings of safety and enjoyment in your classroom is to give them great reasons to be there. If the only time they see the inside of the room is two or three times a year during traditional parent-teacher conferences, it's a fair bet that good times may not be on their minds when they are there. You need to help parents to have good times, opportunities to celebrate and participate in their children's education. If your school has an open house or curriculum night in the first month of school, use the opportunity to put your students "on stage" in the classroom. Have them spend time in the preceding days making things for their families, preparing the classroom in some unusual way for their arrival, writing skits, or writing new lyrics to a familiar song and practicing their performance—anything that will put the kids at the center of the reason for parents to come. Parents who are reluctant to be involved at school may not be remotely tempted to show up if the only reason to do so is to listen to people talk about language arts standards and test results. But if you give their children opportunities to be the ones who do the inviting (e.g., to poetry readings, art shows, science fairs, math games, class plays, family art—even popcorn and movie nights), you'll be giving parents reasons to want to be in your classroom. They will be more likely to want to listen to you talk about your teaching philosophy or to participate in a community conversation about home-work expectations if these kinds of things come second to getting to see their children shine with what they know and can do.

Finally, involve all of your parents by sharing class news on a regular basis with them and highlighting students' collective accomplishments. Send the class's process norms and community norms home in a news-letter, along with an explanation of what you're trying to accomplish with that approach. Write about your philosophy on homework in another newsletter, then hold a potluck/ice cream party some night early in the year so that your students and their parents can talk together and with you about their ideas on homework. (More on this topic in Approach #4 below.) At the same meeting, invite parents to write about their three highest hopes and their three worst fears for the year and then ask them to share their thoughts so they can hear each other's voices. Keep them informed, keep them involved, keep them coming.

Approach #3: Expect that mistakes, misunderstandings, and conflict will be part of the process. Prepare students and parents for this reality.

In building open and healthy relationships with students and parents, your attention must be consciously devoted to the essential value of mistakes, misunderstandings, and failure. In the world of mandated uniformity, errors are punished; only success is rewarded. In this dominant paradigm, being right is of more value than being curi-ous, creative, or tenacious. The progressive educator follows Thomas Edison's lead in welcoming errors as essential to the complex undertak-ing of constructing and reconstructing understandings and discovering new ways of seeing the world. He is said to have explained the value of error by saying, "If I find 10,000 ways something won't work, I haven't failed. I am not discouraged, because every wrong attempt dis-carded is just one more step forward."

The key idea when considering the concept of error in the context of community development, of course, is that mistakes, misunder-standings, and failure can be valuable and productive only when students, parents, and teachers are absolutely convinced that they are in a safe place. People must be secure in the foundation of their rela-tionships with each other to be free to learn from the mistakes they will inevitably make. If you find yourself reluctant to share and discuss your mistakes with your colleagues, students, and parents, one question to consider is whether or not you feel safe with those people. If you don't, you might try to figure out why and whether you can do anything to make it different.

Since prevailing views about education are so firmly devoted to rewarding success and punishing failure, many students and parents may be reluctant to trust your sincerity when it comes to your ability to value mistakes. One way to build this trust is to simply talk with students and parents about the essential role that mistakes play in the learning process. Importantly, you should include adults' mistakes in this discussion, making it clear that the focus is not only on the child's right to err. Parents and teachers who can talk with each other about the predictability of their own mistakes will be in a better position to respond to each other in productive and respectful ways when they happen. Teachers, students, and parents who can admit to each other when they've made mistakes will be demonstrating that blend of confidence and humility that are prerequisites for the growth of genuine authority.

Approach #4: Work to understand the perspectives and motivations of seemingly unreasonable and "difficult" parents.

One of the challenges to building relationships with parents in which mistakes and misunderstandings are anticipated and valued has to do with the different perspectives that parents and teachers bring to bear on a classroom. Naturally, parents focus primarily on the well-being of their own children; the teacher's focus is just as naturally much broader than that. Your perspective requires that you work to balance your concern for each individual child while simultaneously maintaining your focus on the well-being of the class as a whole. While most parents will automatically understand and support you in this without any special effort on your part, it can be hard to get through to a small minority of parents—particularly in the beginning of a new year before relationships are established.

In working with "difficult" parents, we urge educators everywhere to adopt the mind-set that Brendtro, Brokenleg, and Van Bockern (2002) have advocated for people working with "difficult" youth. They prefer to use terms like *discouraged*, *alienated*, *troubled*, and *at-risk* (Brendtro et al., p. 3) when describing children who do not easily succeed in the school environment, because these terms challenge us to go beyond placing responsibility for success and blame for failure squarely on the child's shoulders. Just as thinking of a child as "difficult" can absolve us from feeling responsible for their success, so can our construct of "difficult parents" keep us from understanding the roots of an individ-ual parent's sense of discouragement and alienation in the school setting.

As difficult as it can sometimes be to extend the same kind of understanding and courtesy to adults that we should routinely be extending to the children in our care, we need to recognize the pecu-liarities of the parent-teacher dynamic. Parents are required by law to entrust a large part of their children's social, emotional, and cognitive health and development to our care, and they may have good reason to feel powerless and alienated in their home-school relationships. The parent-teacher relationship has not typically been construed as one of equals, so the ethical burden is on us to do more of the development and maintenance work in our relationships with parents.

When faced with a discouraged, challenging parent, your priority must be to help him to see that you share the same fundamental goals. You want his daughter to be successful in your classroom—to feel safe, valued, powerful, and capable—and you want her to enjoy school. If you can agree on the importance of these basic goals, you will have taken the first step in establishing a collaborative relationship that will help you and the parent to achieve them. You will go even farther in getting these parents on your side, so to speak, if you can understand the reasons behind what might be overly aggressive, demanding, or obnoxious behaviors. If you have done your best to honor parents' authority while asserting your own; if you have tried to understand whether seemingly inappropriate behavior from parents is rooted in an inability to feel safe, valued, powerful, and capable in the context of their child's school experience; and if you have then tried to facilitate parents' access to those needs in their relationship with you, you will have done all that you can.

Approach #5: Recognize the fact that sometimes the problems are bigger than you.

In the same way that it's important for you to recognize that you do not have the knowledge or skills of a therapist when working with children, the same boundary is essential to recognize in your relation-ships with parents. You may be surprised at the kinds of things some parents will share with you, if you are successful in being the good listener that we are urging you to be. It's important to listen and to be supportive, but your job is to do everything in your power to help your parents to understand and to talk through educational issues involving their children.

Another boundary issue has to do with the importance of recognizing inappropriate family dynamics when children are adversely affected and to know when you are incapable of adequately supporting children on your own in these situations. It is important for you to feel comfortable requesting others' help at school when you find yourself out of your depth in dealing with an immediate problem. What do you do, for example, when a parent who appears to be drunk or high wants his child to hop in the car with him at the end of the day? How do you handle a situation in which a parent cruelly chastises her child or speaks to him in a demeaning way in front of you? For any teacher, particularly for one who is new to the profession, it can be hard to know what to do in situations like these. Be assured that, at least in our experience, they don't happen often. Many teachers will never face them. But you should spend some time thinking through what you would do to protect children in such difficult situations and where you would go for help, just in case.

What would you do if faced with the harsh or high parent described above? If you know the chastising mom is normally a very reasonable person who is just having a terrible day, you might interject with a comment like, "You seem frustrated today, Martha. I know Victor's behavior is probably driving you crazy, but this isn't helping him or you. What can I do to help?" Or to the seemingly inebriated dad, "You know I can't let Teresa get in the car with you, John. Who can I call to come and get the two of you?" However, if it's an extreme situation and you're not yet confident of your relationship with parents, or if you don't know the parents and the student involved, invent a reason if needed to get the child away from the situation and into the office with you. Ask your principal and others for help.

Finally, if you suspect abuse or neglect, you are ethically and legally required to report it. If you have not already learned how to detect signs of abuse or about reporting procedures in your district, make an appointment with an administrator and find out. If you wait until you need to know, you might unintentionally complicate an already-difficult situation by asking a child well-intended but inappropriate questions, potentially compromising any subsequent investigation by child support services or other law enforcement authorities.

Approach #6: Broaden the purpose of parent involvement.

The idea that parents' direct involvement is essential for children's success in school is relatively new. Encouraging parents' engagement in their children's education was one of the recommendations of the 1983 report by the National Commission on Excellence in Education, *A Nation at Risk*. The goal is highly appropriate, but the terms of parent involvement as defined in that report and since then are extremely limiting. For over twenty years, parent involvement has been primarily cast in conservative terms, encouraging it for the sole purpose of improving the chances of academic success for parents' own children. A more progressive version of parent involvement would encourage parents of every community to be engaged and involved in the schools to ensure that *all* children—not just their own—have access to excellent resources and educational opportunities. If achieving the ideals of democracy, freedom, and justice for all can be validly presented as some of the reasons that our public schools exist, then parents must be encouraged to engage in discussions that go well beyond the question of their own children's performance.

Inviting parents at the classroom level to join a discussion group in which you facilitate text-based discussions on individual articles or books on education is one way to transform the home-school dynamic and to broaden the terms of parent-teacher discourse. The unwritten rule, of course, is that parents and teachers are not supposed to discuss the policies and politics of school. A progressive educator on the left end of the continuum of educational thought would argue that unless parents and teachers do exactly that, the policies and politics of school will continue to be defined by powers that exist in remote places, far away from classrooms and children. If there is anything that this radical progressive is interested in doing, it is in rewriting the rules so that substantive parent-teacher conversations can be had and decisions can be made in local schools and classrooms—with children's needs in mind.

SUMMARY

Developing significant community relationships with parents requires that teachers pursue a dynamic in which mutual authority is consciously, purposefully honored. This chapter looked at the following strategies for facilitating strong and effective parent-teacher relationships:

- *Do all that you can think of, and then think and do more, to make your parents feel comfortable with you and in their child's classroom.* The great majority of parents feel anything but powerful when they are on your turf. Your challenge is to help them to believe that your classroom is their turf, too.

- *Give parents great reasons to be in your classroom by continually giving their children opportunities to shine there.* Give children opportunities to shine, and you'll be giving parents reasons to want to be in your classroom.

- *Expect that mistakes, misunderstandings, and conflict will be part of the process. Prepare students and parents for this reality.* Mistakes, misunderstandings, and failure can be valuable and productive when people are absolutely convinced that they are in a safe place.

- *Work to understand the perspectives and motivations of seemingly unreasonable and "difficult" parents.* You will go far in getting these parents on your side, so to speak, if you can understand the reasons behind what might be overly aggressive, demanding, or obnoxious behaviors.

- *Recognize the fact that sometimes the problems are bigger than you.* Seek help when parents come to you with problems you are not qualified to address or when you see family dynamics that endanger students' health and safety.

- *Broaden the purpose of parent involvement.* If achieving the ideals of democracy, freedom, and justice are reasons that our public schools exist, then parents must be encouraged to engage in discussions that go well beyond the question of their own children's performance.

7

Holding On: Leading With Heart

> "Dear Teacher, I am a survivor of a concentration camp. My eyes saw what no man should witness. Gas chambers built by learned engineers. Children poisoned by educated physicians. Infants killed by trained nurses. Women and babies shot and burned by high school and college graduates. So I am suspicious of education. My request is that teachers help students become human. Your efforts must never produce learned monsters, skilled psychopaths, educated Eichmanns. Reading, writing, arithmetic are important only if they serve to make our children more humane." (anonymous high school principal as cited in Ginott, 1972, p. 317)
>
> "We must abandon completely the naive faith that school automatically liberates the mind and serves the cause of human progress; in fact, we know that it may serve any cause. [It] may serve tyranny as well as truth, war as well as peace, death as well as life. . . . Whether it is good or evil depends, not on the laws of learning, but on the conception of life and civilization that gives it substance and direction. In the course of history, education has served every purpose and doctrine contrived by man. If it is to serve the cause of human freedom, it must be explicitly designed for that purpose." (Counts as cited in Purpel, 1989, p. xiii)

A great question—asked at the right time by enough people—is a lever that can be used to move the world. When the world is defined in small enough terms (as an individual school or classroom, for example), the questions suggested by the quotes above have large and immediate kinetic potential: What do our schools and classrooms communicate to students about the purpose of education and, therefore, about our conceptions of life and civilization? Is human freedom the cause that our own teaching is explicitly designed to serve? Are our everyday efforts effectively preparing children to live and work with others in what Terry Tempest Williams (2004) called "the open space of democracy"?

Such questions can provoke productive discussion amongst educators, parents, students, and other members of our schools and neighborhoods. Such discussions may be particularly necessary for those of us who fear that educational leadership in today's United States is more genuinely situated in boardrooms and government buildings than in the administrative offices of our schools and districts—a perception that could explain why human resource development rather than human freedom appears to be the most urgent cause that American education is currently designed to serve. For this to change, educational leadership needs to be resituated. Authority must be claimed at the classroom level—right where it matters the most as far as our students, families, and neighborhoods are concerned.

It's an indisputable point: if you have chosen to teach, it is a matter of fact that you have chosen to be a person of influence—a leader. The only things in question on this point are the size of your influential sphere and the degree of significance you will have in the lives of those within it. Another question altogether is what type of leader you will choose to be, which will determine the kind of influence you will have on the people around you.

An amazing amount of energy has been devoted in recent decades to projects that have contributed to the popular illusion that teachers as a whole are disrespected, intellectually impoverished, and impotent people. Education summits have been held at which governors and corporate leaders speak and to which teachers are not invited. Measures have been taken to hold educators accountable for closing the achievement gap, making them objects of rather than subjects in the process of defining the ends and means of accountability. (And in the cart-before-the-horse logic of political and corporate leaders, educators are expected to close the achievement gap alone—as if such things as the yawning health care gap, housing gap, hazard-free environment gap, and any number of other opportunity gaps do not exist for our students. "No excuses," we are told.) Canned, teacher-proofed curricula are purchased and mandated, most often in schools that serve poor children, encouraging many people to believe that education is a job for flunkies whose responsibilities are limited to managing students' behavior and reading from scripted lessons.

Don't fall for it.

Teachers are among the most powerful people in the world—if definitions of real power, genuine authority, and true leadership are applied. Our view is that real leadership grows the potential for authority and power in others and false leadership diminishes it. Real leaders intentionally and continually seek ways to empower the people who are in their care. They naturally want to be recognized for their accomplishments, but they may be even more proud of the accomplishments of those whom they have mentored. Real leaders look for proof of their effectiveness in terms of what they have helped others to achieve. Real power, we believe, is measured in human terms—in the degree of positive significance that a leader holds in the lives of others. It exists in the degree to which that leader is able to help others to find their questions, achieve their goals, and realize their dreams. The influence of real leaders is a living thing, because it can be passed along. False leaders, by contrast, intentionally and continually seek ways to gather power and prestige to themselves. They hoard the material markers of success. Their influence is often coercive, so it dies with them.

Real leadership is within reach of every citizen. It is most particularly and immediately within reach of teachers. In the lives of your current 15 or 30 or 150 students and their families, you are powerful beyond imagining. Whether the people you teach are first graders, sophomores, or student-teachers, you have the power to influence what they read about, think about, write about, and discuss with each other. You can decide how they spend a measure of their life's time. Whether you do this in a way that increases or diminishes students' access to voice and power in your classroom will be the defining factor of your leadership style.

ON BECOMING A "REAL" LEADER

Real leaders have at least four things in common. They have (1) genuine authority, (2) a driving need to establish with others a clear and purposeful vision and an equally strong determination to work with others toward achieving it, (3) high expectations for themselves and for others, and (4) a healthy dose of what C. Douglas Lummis (1996) called "democratic faith" (p. 151).

The first of these we have previously defined as what results when a perfect balance of confidence and humility is achieved. When that mixture is out of balance, authority is lost: too much confidence, and authority gives way to conceit, certainty, and narrow-mindedness; too much humility, and authority gives way to indecisiveness, timidity, and excessive self-doubt. Most of us have had experience with leaders who were either so nice they were useless when a decision needed to be made or so arrogant that the only clearly valued perspective on a problem was their own. It's the combination of strength and uncertainty that makes a leader trustworthy, making real leadership possible. The crucial balance of confidence and humility allows a person to be open-minded enough to value all perspectives when a decision must be made, yet strong enough to ensure to the best of her ability that every decision will ultimately work toward achieving the group's vision.

If authority is the engine, vision is the destination. If there are members of a class, school, district, or university who have no interest in the leader's pronounced destination, the trip will be a pointless waste of time for them—at best. At worst, it will be a hijacking of their time, their work, and their interests by "leaders" who are more interested in imposing an agenda than engaging their people in its creation. Some of these false leaders say things like, "Get on the train or get run over," but not all are as coarse as that. The smoother ones work to get their people's "buy-in." They engage in all kinds of activities to get their employees (or their students or their colleagues) to believe that their voices matter when it comes to defining the destination and the means of getting there—but when buy-in is the goal, it's a sure bet that the decisions that count have already been made. If Carol Gilligan was right, that to have a voice is to be human, then the only *person* on this kind of train is the leader. The others aboard are merely its fuel.

As leaders in our classrooms, of course, the essential question we face is whether we are preparing our students to find and develop their voices. Are our day-to-day efforts aimed at helping children to value and grow thoughtfully, skillfully, and responsibly into their freedom, or are they encouraging children to accept that their lives, their opportunities, and the questions they think about are best left for others to define? Respecting the authority of others is surely essential in a democracy, but there is no democracy if authority isn't equally, purposefully nurtured in ourselves and in those whom we have opportunities to lead. A train with human beings as passengers takes them where they want to go. This means that people in schools—students and educators alike, as well as parents, whenever possible—must be able to participate to a meaningful degree in choosing their goals and evaluating their progress in ways they find useful.

To carry on the metaphor, then, the leader's authority is the engine, and a well-defined vision (i.e., the articulation of what educators, students, and parents are trying to accomplish and why) provides the destination. A whole lot of fuel and the coordination of many separate wheels will be needed to get that train going and then keep it moving on its own power—as opposed to being pushed along from behind by externally applied force, whether or not the wheels and track are in good working order. In our metaphor, high expectations provide the appropriate fuel, and democratic faith will keep the wheels moving together.

The importance of a leader's expectations cannot be overstated. The classic Rosenthal and Jacobson study (1968) illustrated the point. *Pygmalion in the Classroom: Teacher Expectations and Pupils' Intellectual Development* has been both hailed and criticized over the years by educators seeking to understand the relationship between teacher expectations and student achievement; in the decade that followed its publication, several hundred studies were conducted that replicated the "Pygmalion effect" (Rosenthal, 1980).

In the 1960s, Robert Rosenthal was a psychology professor at Harvard University, and Lenore Jacobson was an elementary school principal in San Francisco. Jacobson wrote to Rosenthal after reading an article of his, published in the *American Scientist* in 1963. In it, he had suggested that the phenomenon of a self-fulfilling prophecy that had been proven to be at work in psychological experiments (in which experimenters' expectations were found to influence their subjects' responses) could potentially be applied in classrooms, too; he hypothesized that teachers' expectations would be found to impact students' academic performances. Jacobson was intrigued by the idea and offered her school as a site for testing his theory. What they discovered together rocked the world of education.

They gave an intelligence test to all of the students in Jacobson's elementary school at the beginning of the academic year, but they led teachers to believe that the test was designed to reveal students' academic potential. Then, without yet paying any attention to the test results, they randomly selected 20% of the students. They told the teachers that those particular children had huge potential for intellectual growth and that they could be expected to "bloom" as learners by the end of the year. Eight months later, after returning and retesting all of the children in the school, Rosenthal and Jacobson found that the randomly selected students who were expected to be high achievers showed significantly more growth than the ones who were not identified to their teachers as having great potential. The greater gains made by children who were expected to make more progress were mirrored in teachers' classroom-level evaluations of students' academic and behavioral performances. Teachers reported that "the 'special' students were better behaved, were more intellectually curious, had greater chances for future success, and were friendlier than their nonspecial counterparts" (Newman & Smith, 1999, ¶9). Without intending to, these educators had subtly encouraged the behaviors they expected to see in particular children. "Not only did they spend more time with these students, they were also more enthusiastic about teaching them and unintentionally showed more warmth to them than to the other students" (Newman & Smith, ¶10). Rosenthal and Jacobson had discovered evidence of a causal relationship between imagination and reality in school: expectations impact achievement.

Such findings might put many of us on the defensive, and reasonably so. Surely, we may argue, student success hinges on more complex factors than those of our own expectations. And it's true—there are so many factors in play. Kids who don't have enough food, or sleep, or love, or discipline, or medical and dental attention, or other kinds of support at home come into our classrooms every day with needs that extend far beyond what we can address. But that reality does nothing to lessen the damaging effects on children who—though subtly and unconsciously on our parts—do not enjoy as much of our encouragement, time, enthusiasm, and warmth as some of their peers. Maxine Greene (1993) described the net effect of this unintended harm with the observation that "persons marked as unworthy are unlikely to feel good enough to pose the questions in which learning begins, unlikely to experience whatever curriculum is presented as relevant to their being in the world" (p. 212). Children know when they have been marked as unworthy, and they're usually only too willing to live down to low expectations. The Pygmalion effect works both ways.

Real educational leaders at every level understand how crucial it is for the people in their care to know that they are worthy of high expectations. Unfortunately, low expectations are not only common, they are often institutionally sanctioned through tracking—a practice that is widely used, commonly accepted, and lacking even a basic level of consensus in research literature that it promotes achievement (Hanushek & Woessman, 2005; Oakes & Wells, 1997; Viadero, 2005;

Wheelock, 1992). Fixed ability grouping is at odds with the cause of human freedom for *all* students. This point is effectively illustrated through Anne Wheelock's (1992) description of tracking, read in the light of Rosenthal and Jacobson's findings about self-fulfilling prophecies: "Once sorted and classified, students are provided with curriculum and instruction deemed suited to their ability and matched to spoken or unspoken assessments of each student's future" (Tracking to Untracking section, ¶2). It is arguably clear that the cause of human resource development is served well by principles of school and classroom design that are rooted in the "tracked" values of control—of efficiency, uniformity, and predictability. The cause of human freedom requires something more.

DEMOCRATIC FAITH: THE FINAL, ESSENTIAL COMPONENT OF LEADERSHIP

Through their own authority, real leaders are able to generate trust. Through their ability to facilitate the creation of a clear, worthwhile, and achievable vision, they are able to help others understand their purpose. Because they deeply respect the people in their care, they are able to translate that vision into concrete expectations that cause those people to reach for their best. But authority, vision, and high expectations alone are not enough.

A true educational leader needs to be able to coordinate all of the wheels on the train, so to speak, ensuring that all of the moving parts can work independently but also together, in service to a common goal. That kind of coordination—in which each person is thoroughly supported, trusted to do their part, and included in defining the measures of their own accountability—reflects the unwavering presence of what Lummis (1996) called democratic faith. This he defined as "the decision to believe that a world of democratic trust is possible because we can see it in each person sometimes. It is the decision to believe in what people can be on the basis of what they sometimes are" (p. 154). False leaders have no need of democratic faith; they don't have to be able to trust students, teachers, administrators, and parents, because democracy is not their goal. All they need to be able to impose their will and to coerce obedience is access to compelling rewards and punishments. The deep and jagged gash in the educational landscape that is created from pushing that train along from behind is just another price to pay for "progress," a term that is rarely defined by the people who bear its burden.

Real leaders don't micromanage, and they don't coerce obedience. They cultivate faith. As Lummis (1996) warned us, though, "Democratic faith is not simply trusting everybody equally; it is not sentimental foolishness. It is grounded on a lucid understanding of the weaknesses, follies, and horrors people are capable of. It is precisely because of those weaknesses, follies, and horrors that something so weighty as faith is called for" (p. 154). How might the accountability discourse in education be different today had the past couple of decades been determinedly focused on cultivating something so weighty as a lucid faith in every child's ability to learn? What measures would we now have in place to guide us in ensuring that we have done all that we can to grow our students' *desire* to learn? What effect would accountability measures have on students' cognitive achievements if we decided that the essential accounting is primarily affective (i.e., regarding children's experience of safety, value, competence, autonomy, and enjoyment of challenging work in school)?

Reframing the terms of accountability to promote students' desire to learn, educators' desire to teach, and parents' desire to be involved seems like a logical response to the sense of alienation and demoralization that currently shapes school culture for so many of the teachers and student-teachers we know. Pragmatically, though, a paradigm shift of such monumental proportion is unlikely. Our most powerful leaders do not appear to be devoted to the project of growing authority in others; they seem to lack sufficient faith in children, educators, and families to make that happen. But this needn't keep democratic faith from growing on a smaller scale where it counts the most, in the context of our own classrooms, schools, and neighborhoods.

FROM THEORY TO PRACTICE: STRATEGIES FOR HOLDING ON AND LEADING WITH HEART

Approach #1: Cultivate faith in those around you.

Whether your sphere of influence is defined by the boundaries of your classroom, school, neighborhood, or beyond, the positive influence you will have as an educational leader exists in direct proportion to the degree of faith you demonstrate in the people around you. In the classroom, this means that your students must know that you trust and believe in them, but they also must know that you're not an idiot when it comes to how you show them that faith. Your belief in kids cannot be an exercise in "sentimental foolishness." They need to know that you're sharp, that you can tell when they're playing you, and that the boundaries that you've established together are real and reliable.

You can show your students that you have faith in them by providing them with regular opportunities to make meaningful choices for themselves. Give them responsibility for solving their own problems and for fixing their mistakes by creating clear and dependable structures that are designed to provide support and to facilitate their ownership and authority (e.g., class meetings; norms and rubrics that students help write). Create routines that allow students to be in charge of taking care of their own physical needs and environmental responsibilities. When assessing and evaluating students' knowledge and skills, give them a degree of choice whenever possible about how to demonstrate their understandings. Involve students when you can in the processes of maintaining a positive learning environment, planning activities, assessing what they know and can do, and evaluating and reporting their progress. We do not see student involvement in these processes as *always* feasible, but by sharing real responsibilities with your students regularly and often, you will be letting them know that you trust them, that you value their voices and realities, and that you really do believe that students' mistakes and problems must be owned before education can be achieved.

With colleagues and parents, the cultivation of faith requires the same kind of eyes-wide-open commitment to honoring their capacity for goodness. You can demonstrate a commitment to this belief by trying to ensure that every adult you work with feels genuinely valued by you (whether or not you like or agree with them, or they with you)—not through sentimental foolishness or insincerity but through your determination to hear them and to treat them honorably, whether they're within earshot or not.

Approach #2: Encourage the collaborative development and articulation of high academic and behavioral expectations for every member of your classroom and school, emphasizing the need for each person in the community to cultivate his or her own democratic faith.

Without faith, high expectations are dishonest. Without high expectations, faith is unnecessary. Students, educators, and parents understand when they have been "marked as unworthy" (Greene, 1993, p. 212) of others' high expectations and faith, because instead of knowing that they are safe, valued, capable, and powerful, they feel threatened, unimportant, ineffectual, and controlled. Indeed, this is the fundamental problem that the current standards and accountability movement has created. People who understand that they are unworthy of others' faith have no reason to risk investing their true selves or their best efforts in the classroom.

Helping students, parents, and colleagues to discuss and articulate publicly their highest hopes for themselves and each other in your classroom and school—even if your own leaders are not helping you to feel safe, valued, capable, and powerful—is a positive action that you can take to create space for high expectations and democratic faith in the world as you define it. Simply helping to launch such a conversation would be a step toward the goal of resituating authority, moving it closer to the places where children live.

Approach #3: Join or form a Critical Friends Group at your school or with colleagues from other schools in your area.

Whether they are called Critical Friends Groups, Professional Learning Communities, or Teaching Circles, the idea is the same: educators have joined together for the ongoing purpose of improving their professional knowledge and skills in a supportive, challenging, and collegial environment. This is the single most powerful step we can recommend for teachers who are interested in taking charge of their own professional development by making student achievement its central focus. Educators who join together to form learning communities have safe places in which to work through the challenges they are facing in their practice. This group of advocates will support one another in their mutual goal of helping every student to be successful by engaging in focused observations of each other's teaching, by looking at students' work and helping each other to probe for understanding of what is next for those students to learn, and by pushing one another's thinking about particular dilemmas they are facing in their classroom practice—to name but a few of the functions of this type of learning community for educators. Members of a Critical Friends Group could also use this kind of forum for launching action research projects in their classrooms and school, with members working together to cultivate their skills in posing questions, gathering and analyzing qualitative and quantitative data, and learning about theoretical frameworks that will help them to make sense of their findings.

Teaching can be a lonely profession, particularly for those who are committed to progressive teaching in these regressive times. Finding just a few other people with whom to engage in this kind of focused, productive, professional development can make the difference between being a short-timer or a teacher for life. To get started, find out if any colleagues in your school or district have attended workshops to learn how to form and "coach" a Critical Friends Group. If this is a new idea in your school or district, search online to find out how to get in touch with centers in your area that offer these kinds of opportunities. (The National School Reform Faculty Web site at http://www.harmony school.org/nsrf/default.html is one place to begin such a search.)

Approach #4: Develop the habit of asking productive questions and of encouraging them from your students.

Ira Chaleff, author of *The Courageous Follower: Standing Up to and for Our Leaders* (2003), wrote

> As followers, our formal powers are unequal to the leader's, and we must learn to participate effectively in the relationship despite this. We may have far more power than we imagine, however, and too often fail to exercise the power we do have. It is critical for followers to connect with their power and learn how to use it. To maintain and strengthen power, it must be used; otherwise, it will wither. (p. 48)

We believe, as Chaleff suggested, that each of us is far more powerful than we dare to imagine. Teachers, in particular, who are expected every day to pose questions—levers that can be used to move the world—are in position to shape reality. There is enormous power in being able to ask a good question courteously, focusing our own and others' attention on a productive line of inquiry. The trick is to figure out how to ask genuine questions that invite others to critical conversation rather than to turn people away from the issues we care about by framing our questions through preconceived judgments and attitudes of certainty. Asking administrators and colleagues in a faculty meeting, "Who decided that we should track kids into fixed-ability reading groups for the year, and how dare we stigmatize kids for life in that way?" is more likely to raise defenses than awareness, turning everyone but the people who are already singing in your choir away from the issue about which you care so deeply.

Asking a real question requires our willingness to wonder sincerely with others and not know the answers we are looking for.

Asking, "Can we have a conversation about how each of us is perceiving the benefits and drawbacks of how we've grouped kids for reading?" may not bring about an immediate decision to untrack your school's reading program, but an inviting, genuine question has a greater chance of at least attracting more people to the conversation. It might eventually open the door for study groups to form, each tackling a different book or series of articles about researched effects of different grouping strategies on students' achievements and attitudes. Asking genuine questions courteously is one way for teachers to become subjects in rather than objects of the accountability discourse in our schools, districts, states, and nation. Through critical inquiry, we claim our democratic right to participate in shaping our realities.

Finally, if we want our teaching to serve the cause of human freedom, we need to extend to students the same right to ask critical questions, thus inviting them to participate in shaping their realities in our classrooms. We need to teach them how to ask genuine questions courteously so that they, too, can learn how to invite others to the issues they care about most deeply.

We can begin the work of making our classrooms places in which great questions are asked and pursued by simply recording for a week the questions we hear from our students, and then sharing that list with them. We might even categorize those questions with students using Bloom's taxonomy as our organizational framework, inviting hypotheses to explain why so many of our questions in school tend to cluster around the knowledge and comprehension end of that continuum. We could launch an informal study or a formal unit on great questions that have changed the world, and we could incorporate students' genuine questions into our instructional plan as we try to teach them to be powerful readers, writers, mathematicians, scientists, social scientists, and artists. We can show them that their questions are levers that can move the world.

Approach #5: Hold on to hope.

> Another world is not only possible, she is on her way.
> On a quiet day, I can hear her breathing.
>
> —Arundhati Roy

In the end, teaching is about leading, and leading is ultimately an expression of hope. And hope, according to novelist Barbara Kingsolver (1997), is what life itself is all about. "The very least you can do in your life is to figure out what you hope for," she wrote. "And the most you can do is live inside that hope. Not admire it from a distance but live right in it, under its roof" (p. 299). It is through offering students our faith that our capacity for hope is revealed. It is through living inside of hope and inviting our students, families, and colleagues along that we can find the future we want to grow into together.

SUMMARY

Teachers are leaders with tremendous potential to help others to find their questions, achieve their goals, and realize their dreams. The following strategies will help teachers lead with heart:

- *Cultivate faith in those around you.* The positive influence you will have as an educational leader will exist in direct proportion to the degree of faith you demonstrate in the people around you.
- *Encourage the collaborative development and articulation of high expectations for every member of your classroom and school, emphasizing the need for each person in the community to cultivate their own democratic faith.* Helping students, parents, and colleagues discuss and publicly articulate their highest hopes for themselves and each other is a positive action that you can take to create a space for high expectations and democratic faith.
- *Join or form a Critical Friends Group at your school or with colleagues from other schools.* Such groups provide educators with safe places in which to work through the challenges they are facing in their practice. Group members can support one another in the mutual goal of helping every student to be successful.
- *Develop the habit of asking productive questions and of encouraging them from your students.* There is enormous power in being able to ask genuine questions that invite others to critical conversation.

- *Hold on to hope.* It is through offering students our faith that our capacity for hope is revealed. It is through living inside of hope and inviting our students, families, and colleagues along that we can find the future we want to grow into together.

References

Albuquerque Public Schools. (2001). Curriculum. (Available from Albuquerque Public Schools, 6400 Uptown Boulevard NE, Albuquerque, NM 87110)

Alliance for Excellent Education. (2005, August). Teacher attrition: A costly loss to the nation and to the states. *Issue Brief.* Retrieved April 22, 2006, from www.all4ed.org/publications/TeacherAttrition.pdf

Austin, T. (1994). *Changing the view: Student-led parent conferences.* Portsmouth, NH: Heinemann.

Beale, A., & Yilik-Downer, A. (2001). "Bullybusters": Using drama to empower students to take a stand against bullying behavior. *Professional School Counseling, 4,* 300–306.

Bennett, R. (1993). Influence of behavior perceptions and gender on teachers' judgments of students' academic skill. *Journal of Educational Psychology, 85*(2): 347–356.

Bigelow, B., & Peterson, B. (Eds.). (1991). *Rethinking Columbus: The next 500 years.* Milwaukee, WI: Rethinking Schools.

Booher-Jennings, J. (2006a, October 5). Rationing education. *The Washington Post,* p. A33.

Booher-Jennings, J. (2006b, June). Rationing education in an era of accountability. *Phi Delta Kappan, 87*(10): 756-761. Retrieved June 22, 2007, from www.pdkintl.org/kappan/k_v87/k0606boo.htm

Brendtro, L. K., Brokenleg, M., & Van Bockern, S. (2002). *Reclaiming youth at risk: Our hope for the future.* Bloomington, IN: The Solution Tree.

Brookhart, S. (1994). Teachers' grading: Practice and theory. *Applied Measurement in Education, 7*(4): 279–301.

Caine, R. N. (2004). 12 Brain/mind principles in action: *One author's personal journey.* Retrieved February 8, 2006, from www.newhorizons.org/neuro/caine%202.htm

Caine, R. N., & Caine, G. (1997). *Education on the edge of possibility.* Alexandria, VA: Association for Supervision and Curriculum Development.

Chaleff, I. (2003). *The courageous follower: Standing up to and for our leaders.* San Francisco: Berrett-Koehler Publishers.

Combs, A. W. (1976). What we know about learning and criteria for practice. In S. B. Simon & J. A. Ballanca (Eds.), *Degrading the grading myth: A Primer of*

Alternatives to Grades and Marks. Washington, DC: Association for Supervision and Curriculum Development.

Corbett, D., & Wilson, B. (2002, September). What urban students say about good teaching. *Educational Leadership, 60,* 18–22.

Curwin, R. L. (1976). Dispelling the grading myths. In S. B. Simon & J. A. Ballanca (Eds.), *Degrading the grading myth: A Primer of Alternatives to Grades and Marks.* Washington, DC: Association for Supervision and Curriculum Development.

Daggett, W. (1993, November). *A 100-year history of education in the continental United States.* Address delivered at the General Session of the Alaska Association of School Boards' Annual Conference, Anchorage, Alaska.

Daggett, W. (1998, February). *Academic standards: The need for rigor and relevance.* Presentation at the National Schools Conference Institute's Effective Schools Conference, Phoenix, Arizona.

Deci, E. L., & Koestner, R. (1999). A meta-analytic review of experiments examining the effects of extrinsic rewards on intrinsic motivation. *Psychological Bulletin,* 125(6), 627–669.

Deci, E. L., & Ryan, R. M. (n.d.). *Self-Determination Theory: An approach to human motivation & personality.* Retrieved August 19, 2005, from www.psych.roche ster.edu/SDT/

Deci, E. L., & Ryan, R. M. (1996). Need satisfaction and the self-regulation of learning. *Learning & Individual Differences,* 8(3), 165–184.

Deci, E. L., & Ryan, R. M. (2000). The "what" and "why" of goal pursuits: Human needs and the self-determination of behavior. *Psychological Inquiry,* 11(4), 227–269.

Delpit, L. (2006). *Other people's children: Cultural conflict in the classroom* (Rev. ed.). New York: The New Press.

Dewey, J. (1989). *Freedom and culture.* Amherst, NY: Prometheus Books. (Original work published 1939)

Dewey, J. (1997a). *Democracy and education.* New York: Simon and Schuster. (Original work published 1916)

Dewey, J. (1997b). *Experience and education.* New York: Touchstone. (Original work published 1938)

Garrity, C., Jens, K., Porter, W., Sager, N., & Short-Camilli, C. (1997). Bully-proofing your school: Creating a positive climate. *Intervention in School & Clinic,* 32, 235–244.

Gilligan, C. (1982). *In a different voice: Psychological theory and women's development.* Cambridge, MA: Harvard University Press.

Ginott, H. (1972). *Teacher and child: A book for parents and teachers.* New York: The Macmillan Company.

Gladwell, M. (2002). *The tipping point: How little things can make a big difference.* Boston: Little, Brown, and Company.

Glasser, W. (1998a). *Choice Theory: A new psychology of personal freedom.* New York: HarperCollins.

Glasser, W. (1998b, February). *Choice Theory in the schools.* Keynote address at the National School Conference Institute's Effective Schools Conference, Phoenix, Arizona.

Graham, S. (1995, January). *Authentic tasks.* Presentation at the National School Conference Institute's Effective Schools Conference, Phoenix, Arizona.

Greene, M. (1993). Diversity and inclusion: Toward a curriculum for human beings. *Teachers College Record, 95*(2), 210–221.

Greene, M. (1995). *Releasing the Imagination.* San Francisco: Jossey-Bass Publishers.

Guskey, T. R. (1994). Making the grade: What benefits students? *Educational Leadership, 52*(2), 14–20.

Guskey, T. R. (1996). Reporting on student learning: Lessons from the past, prescriptions for the future. In T. R. Guskey (Ed.), *Communicating Student Learning.* Alexandria, VA: Association for Supervision and Curriculum Development.

Hanushek, E. A., & Woessmann, L. (2005, February). *Does educational tracking affect performance and inequality? Differences-in-differences evidence across countries* [abstract] (Working Paper No. 11124). Cambridge, MA: National Bureau of Economic Research. Retrieved February 11, 2006, from http://papers.nber.org/papers/

Hatter, S. (1978). Pleasure derived from challenge and the effects of receiving grades on children's difficulty level choices. *Child Development, 49*(3), 788–799. Retrieved February 9, 2006, from Academic Search Premier

Hazler, R. J., & Carney, J. V. (2000). When victims turn aggressors: Factors in the development of deadly school violence. *Professional School Counseling, 4*(2), 105–112.

Jacobs, H. H. (1989). *Interdisciplinary curriculum: Design and implementation.* Alexandria, VA: Association for Supervision and Curriculum Development.

Jacobs, H. H. (1997). *Mapping the big picture: Integrating curriculum and assessment K–12.* Alexandria, VA: Association for Supervision and Curriculum Development.

Jacobs, H. H. (2002). Integrated curriculum design. In J. T. Klein (Ed.), *Interdisciplinary education in K–12 and college.* New York: The College Board.

Jensen, E. (1995). *The learning brain.* San Diego, CA: The Brain Store.

Jensen, E. (1998). *Teaching with the brain in mind.* Alexandria, VA: Association for Supervision and Curriculum Development.

John Dewey Project on Progressive Education. (2002). *A brief overview of progressive education.* Burlington, VT: University of Vermont College of Education and Social Services. Retrieved January 7, 2006, from www.uvm.edu/~dewey/articles/proged.html

Kingsolver, B. (1997). *Animal dreams.* New York: Buccaneer Books, Inc.

Kohl, H. (1994). *I won't learn from you: And other thoughts on creative maladjustment.* New York: The New Press.

Kohn, A. (1993). *Punished by rewards.* Boston: Houghton Mifflin Company.

Kohn, A. (1994). Grading: The issue is not how, but why. *Educational Leadership, 52*(2), 38–41.

Kohn, A. (1999). *The schools our children deserve: Moving beyond traditional classrooms and "tougher standards."* Boston: Houghton Mifflin Company.

Kotulak, R. (1997). *Inside the brain: Revolutionary discoveries of how the mind works.* Kansas City, MO: Andrews McMeel Publishing.

Kutner, L. (1991). *Parent and child: Getting through to each other.* New York: William Morrow and Company, Inc.

Lawrence-Lightfoot, S. (2003). *The essential conversation: What parents and teachers can learn from each other.* New York: Random House.

Leff, S., Left, S., Patterson, C., Kupersmidt, J., & Power, T. (1999). Factors influencing teacher identification of peer bullies and victims. *School Psychology Review,* 28(3), 505–518.

Lindquist, T. (2002). *Seeing the whole through social studies* (2nd ed.). Portsmouth, NH: Heinemann.

Lummis, C. D. (1996). *Radical democracy.* Ithaca, NY: Cornell University Press.

Marlowe, B. A., & Page, M. L. (2005). *Creating and sustaining the constructivist classroom.* Thousand Oaks, CA: Corwin Press.

Maslow, A. H. (1943). A theory of human motivation. *Psychological Review,* 50, 379–396. Retrieved July 10, 2007, from http://psychclassics.yorku.ca/Maslow/motivation.htm

McCusker, C. (2002, September 9). Homeschoolers arrive on campus. *Insight on the News,* Newsworld Communications, Inc. Retrieved July 10, 2007, from http://findarticles.com/p/articles/mi_m1571/is_33_18/ai_91475071

McEwan, B. (2000). *The art of classroom management: Effective practices for building equitable learning communities.* Upper Saddle River, NJ: Merrill.

Michigan Department of Education. (2002, March). *What research says about parent involvement in children's education.* Retrieved October 21, 2005, from www.michigan.gov/documents/Final_Parent_Involvement_Fact_Sheet_1472_7.pdf

Mulrine, A. (1999, June 22). Schools target violence by putting a brake on bullies. *Christian Science Monitor,* p. 15.

National Education Association. (2006, May 2). National Teacher Day spotlights key issues facing profession: NEA addresses top five teaching trends and outlines *"Portrait of American Teacher."* Retrieved May 9, 2006, from www.nea.org/newsreleases/2006/nr060502.html

National School Reform Faculty. (n.d.). Retrieved October 1, 2006, from www.nsrfharmony.org

Nelson, J., Lott, L., & Glenn, S. (2000). *Positive discipline in the classroom* (3rd ed.) New York: Random House.

Newman, D. M., & Smith, R. (1999). Building reality: The social construction of knowledge: Sociologists at work: Robert Rosenthal and Lenore Jacobson; Pygmalion in the classroom. In *Sociology: Exploring the Architecture of Everyday Life* (4th ed.; D. M. Newman & J. O'Brien, eds.). Thousand Oaks, CA: Pine Forge Press. Retrieved February 10, 2006, from www.pineforge.com/newman4study/resources/rosenthal1.htm

Northwest Regional Education Library (NWREL). (n.d.). *6+1 trait® writing.* Retrieved October 26, 2005, from www.nwrel.org/assessment/department.php?d=1

Nottingham, M. (1988). Grading practices: Watching out for land mines. *NASSP Bulletin,* 72(507), 24–28.

Oakes, J., & Wells, A. S. (1997). Detracking: The social construction of ability, cultural politics, and resistance to reform. *Teachers College Record, 98*(3). Retrieved February 11, 2006, from Academic Search Premier.

Ohanian, S. (2002). *What happened to recess and why are our children struggling in kindergarten?* New York: McGraw-Hill.

Palmer, P. (1993). *To know as we are known: Education as a spiritual journey.* San Francisco: Harper.

Parker, W. C. (Ed.). (1996). *Educating the democratic mind.* Albany, NY: State University of New York Press.

Perrone, V. (1991) *A letter to teachers: Reflections on schooling and the art of teaching.* San Francisco: Jossey Bass Publishers.

Purpel, D. E. (1989). *The moral and spiritual crisis in education: A curriculum for justice and compassion in education.* New York: Bergin & Garvey Publishers.

Rogers, S. (1995, January). *To grade or not to grade.* Presentation at the National School Conference Institute's Effective Schools Conference, Phoenix, Arizona.

Rogers, S. (1998, February). *Increasing student motivation to learn.* Presentation at the National School Conference Institute's Effective Schools Conference, Phoenix, Arizona.

Rogers, S. (1999). *Teaching tips: 105 ways to increase motivation & learning.* Evergreen, CO: Peak Learning Systems, Inc.

Rogers, S., Ludington, J., & Graham, S. (1997). *Motivation and learning: A teacher's guide to building excitement for learning & igniting the drive for quality.* Evergreen, CO: Peak Learning Systems, Inc.

Rosenthal, R. (1980, February 18). Citation Classic: Pygmalion in the classroom; Teacher expectation and pupils' intellectual development [Electronic version]. *Current Contents: Social & Behavioral Sciences* (7), 12. Retrieved February 11, 2006, from http://garfield.library.upenn.edu/classics.html

Rosenthal, R., & Jacobson, L. (1968). *Pygmalion in the classroom: Teacher expectation and pupils' intellectual development.* New York: Holt, Rinehart & Winston.

Ryan, R. M., & Deci, E. L. (2000). Self-determination theory and the facilitation of intrinsic motivation, social development, and well-being. *American Psychologist, 55*(1), 68–79.

Sapon-Shevin, M. (1999). *Because we can change the world.* Needham Heights, MA: Allyn & Bacon.

Schmidt, W. H., McKnight, C. C., & Raizen S. A. (1997). *A splintered vision: An investigation of U.S. science and mathematics education.* Boston: Kluwer Academic Publishers.

Seligman, M. (1991). *Learned optimism.* New York: A. A. Knopf.

Sheldon, K. M., & Biddle, B. J. (1998). Standards, accountability, and school reform: Perils and pitfalls. *Teachers College Record, 100*(1), 164–181.

Spear, M. (1997). The influence of contrast effects upon teachers' marks. *Educational Research, 39*(2), 229–233.

Sprouse, J. (1994). *The Pygmalion Effect and its influence on the grading and gender assignment on spelling and essay assessments.* Master's thesis, University of Virginia. (ERIC Accession Number ED374096)

Starch, D., & Elliott, E. C. (1912). Reliability of the grading of high school work in English. *School Review, 20,* 442–457.

Starch, D., & Elliott, E. C. (1913). Reliability of grading work in mathematics. *School Review,* 21, 254–295.

Strachota, B. (1996). *On their side: Helping children take charge of their learning.* Turner Falls, MA: Northeast Foundation for Children (NEFC).

Sylwester, R. (1995). *A celebration of neurons: An educator's guide to the human brain.* Alexandria, VA: Association for Supervision and Curriculum Development.

Tempest Williams, T. (2004). *The open space of democracy.* Great Barrington, MA: The Orion Society.

Tomlinson, C. A. (1999). *The differentiated classroom: Responding to the needs of all learners.* Alexandria, VA: Association for Supervision and Curriculum Development.

U.S. Census Bureau. (2005, March 28). *College degree nearly doubles annual earnings.* Retrieved February 7, 2006, from www.census.gov/Press-Release/www/releases/archives/education/004214.html

Vansteenkiste, M., Simons, J., Lens, W., Sheldon, K. M., & Deci, E. L. (2004). Motivating learning performance, and persistence: The synergistic effects of intrinsic goal contents and autonomy-supportive contexts. *Journal of Personality & Social Psychology,* 87(2), 246–260.

Viadero, D. (2005). Report roundup: Academic tracking. *Education Week, 24* (26), 10.

Weinstein, C. S., & Mignano, A. J. (2007). *Elementary classroom management: Lessons from research and practice.* (4th ed.) New York: McGraw-Hill.

Weir, E. (2001). The health impact of bullying. *Canadian Medical Association Journal,* 165(9), 1249.

Wheelock, A. (1992). Crossing the tracks: How "untracking" can save America's schools. Introduction to *Crossing the tracks: How "untracking" can save America's schools.* New York: New Press. Retrieved February 11, 2006, from www.middleweb.com/Whlcktrack.html

Wolfe, P. (2001). *Brain matters: Translating research into classroom practice.* Alexandria, VA: Association for Supervision and Curriculum Development.

Woodward, J. (1997, April 21). The criminal bully reconsidered. *Alberta Report/ Newsmagazine, 24,* 31–32.

Zull, J. (2002). *The art of changing the brain: Enriching the practice of teaching by exploring the biology of learning.* Sterling, VA: Stylus Publishing.

Index

CORWIN PRESS